# WE FELL IN Love

## SHORT STORIES AND POETRY

## SANDRA L. BOBBITT

BOOKSIDE Press

BOOKSIDE Press

BookSide Press
877-741-8091
www.booksidepress.com
orders@booksidepress.com

# CONTENTS

**My Last Pony Ride**

Introduction ........................................................... 10
Chapter One .......................................................... 11
Chapter Two .......................................................... 15
Chapter Three ....................................................... 19
Chapter Four........................................................ 24
Chapter Five ......................................................... 26
Chapter Six........................................................... 34
Chapter Seven ...................................................... 36
Chapter Eight ....................................................... 38
Chapter Nine ........................................................ 40
Chapter Ten.......................................................... 42
Chapter Eleven ..................................................... 46
Chapter Twelve ..................................................... 50
Chapter Thirteen ................................................... 54
Chapter Fourteen .................................................. 56
Chapter Fifteen ..................................................... 58
Chapter Sixteen..................................................... 60
Chapter Seventeen ................................................ 62
Chapter Eighteen................................................... 65
Chapter Nineteen.................................................. 68
Chapter Twenty..................................................... 69
Chapter Twenty-One.............................................. 70
Chapter Twenty-Two.............................................. 72
Chapter Twenty-Three ........................................... 75
Epilogue............................................................... 78

## When Love Comes to Us

Introduction ........................................................ 81
Chapter One ...................................................... 82
Chapter Two ...................................................... 89
Chapter Three ................................................... 92
Chapter Four..................................................... 96
Chapter Five ................................................... 103
Chapter Six..................................................... 107
Chapter Seven ................................................ 109
Chapter Eight ................................................. 111
Chapter Nine .................................................. 113
Chapter Ten.................................................... 117
Chapter Eleven .............................................. 121
Chapter Twelve .............................................. 124
Chapter Thirteen ............................................ 130
Chapter Fourteen ........................................... 133
Chapter Fifteen .............................................. 139
Chapter Sixteen.............................................. 142
Chapter Seventeen ......................................... 147
Chapter Eighteen............................................ 153
Chapter Nineteen............................................ 156
Chapter Twenty............................................... 159
Chapter Twenty-One....................................... 163

## Seven Kittens

Introduction .................................................... 177
Chapter One .................................................... 178
Chapter Two .................................................... 180
Chapter Three ................................................. 182
Chapter Four................................................... 185
Chapter Five ................................................... 190
Chapter Six..................................................... 192
Chapter Seven ................................................ 194
Chapter Eight ................................................. 195
Chapter Nine .................................................. 198
Chapter Ten.................................................... 201
Chapter Eleven ............................................... 204

**Just Charlie Knows**

Introduction ........................................................ 209
Chapter One ...................................................... 210
Chapter Two ...................................................... 214
Chapter Three ................................................... 216
Chapter Four...................................................... 219
Chapter Five ...................................................... 221
Chapter Six........................................................ 228
Chapter Seven .................................................. 233
Chapter Eight ................................................... 237
Chapter Nine .................................................... 240
Chapter Ten...................................................... 242
Chapter Eleven ................................................. 244
Chapter Twelve ................................................. 249
Chapter Thirteen ............................................... 251
Epilogue............................................................ 253

**Moonbeams and Fireflies**

Our Love............................................................ 255
Some Say........................................................... 256
First Anniversarry .............................................. 257
Broken Heart ..................................................... 258
Angels Came For You ....................................... 259
I Am Lonesome................................................. 260
Calls of the Earth .............................................. 261
Moonbeams and Fireflies................................. 262
The Search for Love .......................................... 263
The Eagle Soars................................................ 264
Nature's Songs.................................................. 265
My Special Stars................................................ 266
Alone at Christmas............................................ 267
The World Was Mine to Have............................ 268
A Life Once Shared........................................... 269
Widowhood ...................................................... 271
You Are Here...................................................... 272
The Final Love Story .......................................... 273
Epilogue............................................................ 275

# When Love Comes

*We have loved,*
*We have been loved,*
*We have been lovers,*
*We have lost love,*
*We have found love again.*

ALSO BY SANDRA BOBBITT

Life's Little Bumps and Glitches: A Book of Poetry
I Had a Dream: Student Nurse to Nurse Practitioner
A Heroine's Journey: An Adventure In Self-Reflection
Coming Home: A Road to Healing
Occupational Health and Safety: Fundamentals for
the California Human Resource Professional

# My Last Pony Ride

# Introduction

When we moved to Summit Grove, a small town in Central Arizona, my husband and I thought we would live out our lives in this slow-paced community. A year later, my husband had a massive heart attack and died. The love of my life was gone and I was bereaved.

One hot day in July, a friend of mine, Jenny, called. "I would like to introduce you to someone."

"I don't know," I said hesitantly. "I'm not sure I am ready to go out with anyone yet."

"Rex is a very nice man and was recently widowed. It's time you started going out and you will do just fine," Jenny said. "How about meeting me and my boyfriend at the senior center dance on Saturday. I know Rex will be there and I could introduce you to him."

I thought for a moment and decided that I had nothing to lose. "Okay, but only if you are there."

# Chapter One

I wasn't sure if I wanted to meet Jenny's friend. I had just turned seventy and it seemed all of the men I met my age looked and acted old. Regardless of how I felt and thought, I took extra time getting dressed on Saturday.

At six o'clock, I walked into the senior center. I was dressed in my usual western attire which consisted of a pair of black jeans with bling down the legs, a red shirt with more bling, a red hat and red boots. I saw Jenny and her boyfriend, Jim, and made my way through the crowded room. As I approached them, I gave them both a hug and kiss on the cheek. It was then that I noticed a tall, handsome cowboy standing off to the side. My heart did a flip flop and I'm sure I turned three shades of red. "Roxie this is Rex and Rex this is Roxie," Jenny said as she introduced us.

I reached out my hand to shake Rex's hand, or at least this is what I remember doing. I was locked into Rex's deep blue eyes. The spell was broken when I heard Jenny say, "Let's sit down and wait for the band to return from their break."

Like children responding to a parent's command, we sat down at a table for four. In a deep, soft voice, Rex asked what I would like to drink.

"A glass of Chardonnay would be great," I said feeling like a young school girl.

"I'll be right back with drinks." I watched Rex as he walked away and noticed his somewhat sexy gait.

"Why didn't you tell me he was so damn good looking?" I asked Jenny.

"You didn't ask me," Jenny said smiling.

Rex was a tall man. I would guess he stood over 6'2" and he had a certain presence about him. His eyes were a piercing blue and his face was tanned as if he had spent years outside.

When Rex returned with our drinks, we didn't have time to start a conversation because the band had returned and started their next set. "I hope you western dance," Rex said as he put his arm on the back of my chair leaning forward close to my ear.

"Yes, I do." I replied breathlessly.

"Then may I have this dance?"

The band was playing a popular western slow song and after a few awkward steps, Rex smiled and said, "I think you are leading."

"Oops, I believe you're right," I laughed. "Tell me what you are doing and I will do my best to follow." Rex was a good dancer and when I let him lead, I was soon able to follow him without stepping on his feet.

After a couple of dances, we sat down. The band had gotten so loud it was difficult to hear each other talk. "Have you had dinner?" Rex asked. I simply shook my head 'no' so I wouldn't have to scream over the band.

"Let's get out of here and go somewhere where we can get a bite to eat and talk." I was in total agreement. As we left, we waved goodbye to Jenny and Jim.

"How about I follow you to the restaurant," I offered not wanting to be without my car when we had just met.

"Great. There is a little Mexican restaurant down the road. I'll meet you there." The restaurant was a short mile away and Rex was waiting for me by his truck when I arrived. As he opened my car door, he gave me one of his wonderful smiles.

"Have you eaten here before?" he asked as we walked to

the restaurant.

"No, I haven't," I replied as I felt tingles down to my toes when Rex put his hand ever so gently on the small of my back.

The waitress greeted us and called Rex by name. "Hi Rosa. There will be two of us. Do you have a quiet table?"

"We have a table by the window that has just been vacated and there is no one else seated in this section. Just give me a moment to clear the table."

"That was nice of her." I said.

We didn't say anything else waiting for the table to be cleared. Perhaps I made a mistake, I thought.

Rosa returned and led us to the table. Once again Rex placed his hand on the small of my back and I felt electric sparks from his touch. OK, so this just might be alright.

We ordered drinks. Rex ordered a beer and I had another glass of wine. Rosa brought our drinks and asked if we were ready to order.

"We're in no hurry." Rex said asking her to return come back in ten or fifteen minutes.

"Well, here's to meeting," Rex held up his beer I met his glass in a toast.

We talked for a long time over drinks and dinner. I learned that he was a cattle rancher and had a rather large spread east of Summit Grove. He had been married for thirty years and his wife died two years ago of breast cancer. He had no children

"Tell me about yourself," Rex smiled. "I've been doing all of the talking."

"Well, I've been in Summit Grove for two years. My husband died shortly after we moved. We had planned to retire here."

Rex offered the usual condolences. "What kind of work did you do? I assume you had a career."

"I was a professor for the university and taught music. I had always wanted to be a musician, but I couldn't earn a living playing and singing. So, I got my degree in music theory when I was forty years old and was fortunate enough to get a job with the university."

"What instruments do you play?"

"I mainly play the piano and guitar and dabble on the drums.

"What kind of music do you play?"

I can play anything from classical to western."

"That's why you like to western dance and dress the way you do."

"Well, I'm sort of a wanna-be cowgirl."

"Hmm. What are your other talents?"

"I'm a great cook and love to entertain."

"I love to eat so we have something in common." We both laughed.

Rex was very easy to talk to and I found I didn't want the evening to end. Rosa had returned to tell us that the restaurant was closing.

Walking out, Rex said smiling, "I'd like to see you again. The rodeo starts at the fairgrounds tomorrow. Would you be interested in going, say around six o'clock?"

I was delighted I would be seeing Rex again. "I love rodeos and I'll meet you tomorrow at the fairgrounds."

# Chapter Two

Why is it women spend so damn much time deciding what to wear? I was to meet Rex in two hours and had tried on at least five outfits. Damn those extra pounds I put on over the past year. Well, it is only a rodeo and bound to be hot and dusty.

I finally settled on a blue western shirt. Blue brings out my blue eyes, I rationalized. I put on my favorite blue jeans, boots, western hat and belt. I left the bling at home, although I felt sort of naked without it.

Two hours later, I was at the fairgrounds looking for Rex. He would not be difficult to find with his tall stature and tanned face. Before I spotted him, I heard a sexy male voice say, "Hello cowgirl."

I turned around to find Rex standing behind me.

"Well, hello cowboy," I laughed.

"All you need is a gun and a horse," Rex told me.

"I don't have a horse, but I do have guns."

"You surely do surprise me."

I had grown up attending rodeos in the Midwest, so they weren't foreign to me. We were at the entry gate and I wondered if Rex was going to buy tickets at the ticket booth.

"Don't worry, Darl'n. I have reserved VIP seats each year. Come with me." OK, so I was impressed as Rex held my arm and led me through the crowd to the VIP seating section.

We had seats in the front row and arrived just as the fireworks announced the start of the night performances. A cowgirl trick rider rode atop her white horse adorned in a white western outfit complete with bling and fringe. She rode around the arena as she held the American flag while the band played the "Star Spangled Banner." It was truly a site to behold. The crowd was wild with applause and the rodeo was officially underway.

The first competition was tie-down roping. As we watched, the calf was released from the chute and the roper and his horse took off in hot pursuit. The cowboy swung his rope over his head and expertly launched it around the calf's neck. When the horse came to a halt, the roper dismounted, ran to the calf, flipped it over and tied its legs.

Half way through the tie-down roping, a cute waitress wearing a skimpy pair of jean shorts and t-shirt came to ask if we wanted drinks or something to eat. "Now I know why you like these seats," I said giving Rex a poke in the side.

Rex didn't say anything, only smiled. "What would you like to drink?"

"A cold beer would be wonderful." It was seven o'clock at night and the temperature lingered in the eighties.

Next, we watched saddle bronc riding. This was always a hard event for me to watch with the horse bucking and the cowboy hanging on for dear life. I could visualize the force exerted on the cowboy's spine.

"Can we take a break and walk around a little?" I asked after watching three cowboys being thrown from a bronc.

"Sure, I'll pick up a program for us."

We found a young cowgirl selling programs and Rex paid for the program and handed it to me. Leafing through the pages, I stopped at the team roping section and scanned the entrants.

"Oh, My Gosh," I replied stopping to re-read the cowboy's names. "I know one of the cowboys in the team roping event. We need to stay and see him compete."

"Works for me."

We returned to our seats just as the team roping started. "Just who is this person you know?"

"Brad worked at the university in the agricultural division. He used to talk to me about the early ranching days of Arizona. He runs cattle here and in Montana."

Just then, the announcer called Brad's name and I was on the front of my seat. Brad was positioned to the left of the steer with his partner to the right. The chute opened and the steer ran out with Brad and his partner behind him. Brad threw his rope around both horns and his partner threw his rope around the steer's back legs. They had a time of 7.5 seconds. Not a bad time, but not good enough to win the event.

I was bursting with excitement, "That was amazing." I said turning to Rex. He was smiling and asked, "Would you like to talk with your cowboy?"

"Yes, but how will we find him?"

"I have a few connections. We will find him as soon as they announce the winners."

After the winners were announced, we left our seats and fought the crowd to the opposite side of the arena where the stock animals were kept. Rex eyed one of the arena crew members, whistled as only men can do, and waved his friend to us.

"Jeff, this is Roxie and she has a friend that just finished the team roping event and wants to talk with him. Can you help us out?"

"Sure, what's his name and I will find him."

Jeff wasn't gone long before I saw this dusty, middle-aged, bowl-legged, bald headed cowboy saunter in our direction. When he recognized me, he broke into a run and gave me a big bear hug.

"Roxie, what are you doing here? I heard you moved, but no one seemed to know where."

"Brad, this is my friend Rex." The men shook hands in a friendly gesture.

"I've been here for two years. My husband died shortly after we moved."

"I'm sorry to hear that, Roxie." Brad put his hat back on his head, mostly because he seemed uncomfortable and needed something to do.

"How long are you in town?" I asked.

"I leave tonight for another rodeo in southern Arizona."

"If I give you my phone number, will you promise to keep in touch?"

"It's a promise. Sorry I can't visit longer, but I need to get on the road."

"He seems like a nice fellow."

"Yes, he is and it was great to meet up with him again." I knew Brad wouldn't keep in touch, but I felt better making the effort.

"Come on, let's get out of here. I'm hungry, how about you?"

We drove to a little out of the way hamburger place and had the best burger and fries ever. The night was getting late. Rex took me back to my car and we made plans to go western dancing at the Chick Saloon on Saturday night, just two nights away.

"Will you let me pick you up, say about six o'clock?"

We had been together on two occasions and I generally wouldn't let anyone know where I lived so early in a relationship. Before I knew it I was saying, "That would be great." Oh well, so much for protocol.

# Chapter Three

Here I go again, as I agonized over what to wear. I had never been to Chick's but I heard it was an upscale western bar. That meant bling and perhaps a new outfit. After surveying my wardrobe, I settled on looking for a new outfit. I drove downtown to Sissy's, a high-end western store. Sissy, the owner, was working when I arrived.

"Hi Roxie, what brings you in today?"

"I met a cowboy and we are going to Chick's on Saturday night. I want something new a little sexy."

"This guy must be pretty special."

"I've only been with him twice, but I am hoping to see more of him."

We searched through her racks of jeans, shirts, skirts and dresses. Nothing seemed to jump out at me.

"Just a minute," Sissy said. "I got in a new shipment yesterday and there is something I think you will like."

Sissy left me to re-consider her racks of clothes. Minutes later she returned with a black jumpsuit with bling, lots of bling. I tried it on and immediately knew I would buy it. Bling was sewn down the legs of the pants. The top was sleeveless, partially backless and the entire outfit fit like a glove.

"Sissy, this is fabulous," I said with a big grin as I turned around to see the back in the three-way mirror. "What accessories?"

"Of course, your boots should be black. Add a black western

hat with a rhinestone hat band. Top it off with some flashy earrings and necklace and you will look stunning." Sissy rattled off these items quickly knowing I would ask to see what she had. I walked out of the store having spent several hundred dollars but confident I would feel terrific.

I spent a great deal of time on Saturday preparing for my date with Rex. I had a manicure and pedicure in the morning and came home to a hot Jacuzzi. Make up has never taken me long in the past, but I spent extra time with the details of covering up the age spots that I had begun to acquire. My long hair was brushed to a shine and pulled back behind my ears. Finally, I was ready to put on my new outfit. When I looked into my full-length mirror, I saw a vision I was happy with.

It was five o'clock and Rex was not coming for another hour. To pass the time, I got out my guitar and my favorite western music. The time went quickly and before I knew it, the doorbell rang.

Putting down the guitar, I opened the door. What a vision of manliness I saw. Rex looked like something out of G magazine with his crisp white western shirt and jeans with a pressed front seam. All of this was topped off with a perfectly fitting western hat. Mostly what I saw was his tan chiseled face that showed years of being outside, yet was kind. Lastly, there were those piercing blue eyes that captivated me from the first time we met.

"Well, Darl'n, you look absolutely beautiful." I loved it when he called me Darl'n and could feel myself blush like a young girl at his compliment.

"Was that you playing when I got here?"

"Yes, it was."

"Would you play something for me?"

I was thrilled Rex was interested in my music. My late husband mostly tolerated my playing.

"Would you like a drink first?"

"If you have a little whiskey that would suit me fine."

Knowing he drank whiskey I had picked up a bottle of Jack Daniel's that morning. "On the rocks, right?"

He nodded and I fixed drinks, whiskey for both of us.

Rex was attentive as I played and sang.

"We had better finish our drinks and go, otherwise I could stay and listen to you play and sing all night."

We walked outside in the warm air. I was glad for the sleeveless outfit I was wearing. I looked around for his black truck when he led me to a bright canary yellow Porsche.

"Is this your car?" I asked as he opened the car door for me.

"Yes, Mam. This is my going out car. I use the truck for the ranch."

"Well, it's adorable."        I was feeling very much like a princess.

Summit Grove is a cowboy town and has several western bars. I hadn't been to the Chick Saloon but had seen it from the outside and it was somewhat non-descript.

"Have you been to Chick's before," Rex asked while we drove in excess of the speed limit by ten miles.

"Nope," admiring the expertise he had driving this little yellow car.

"I think you'll like it. The outside is nothing, but the inside is pretty spectacular."

It was seven o'clock when we arrived and the parking lot was nearly full. Rex found an out of the way parking spot. I am sure he parked there to protect his car.

As soon as Rex opened the door to the saloon, we were blasted with noise. "I warned you that it is noisy, but the bands are great."

We walked around the singles and couples sitting at tables and others mingling in the aisles looking for a vacant place to sit. "There's a table over by the wall. Let's go snag it." I followed on Rex's footsteps, a feat in itself since he had a very long gait.

"This place is incredible. It reminds me of Gilley's in Texas." I commented sitting down. There was an enormous dance floor that showed years of use and the lights were reminiscent of Las Vegas. In one corner was a mechanical bull, not something I was interested in trying. In another corner, there were ten or twelve pool tables.

"This is exciting. When does the band start?"

"They start playing at six o'clock and must be on break. What would you like to drink?"

"Sounds like a cold beer kind of an evening."

"I'll be right back."

Rex returned a few minutes later with two beers and cold, frosty glasses. He also managed to bring back an order of nachos. "A little nutritional snack while we wait."

"And we will burn off the calories. Right?"

"I plan to dance off that little fanny of yours, so dig in."

The evening was incredible. We danced nearly every dance and our feet were in perfect step when we danced to the slow dances.

By ten o'clock I was tired and my feet were killing me. "You look tired," Rex confirmed my aching feet.

"I am, but I don't want to end the evening so soon. Would you like to come over for a drink or coffee?"

"A cup of coffee would be good before I start the hour drive back to the ranch."

We didn't talk much on the way home and I was pleased that Rex was comfortable with silence. Once we got to my house, he was ever the gentleman and opened doors for me. I put on a pot of coffee and while it was brewing, he asked me to play the piano. I was only too willing to oblige him.

"What would you like to hear?" Rex surprised me when he asked for a classical piece. I decided upon Fur Elise and when I finished, I looked up and saw Rex reclining back with his eyes closed. "That was beautiful," he remarked looking at me.

I served the coffee and we sat on the sofa talking. Before we knew it, it was two in the morning.

"I need to go home before the sun comes up," he said laughing.

"Are you OK to drive home? I was concerned but not ready to suggest he stay the night.

"I am okay. The coffee helped." He got up, stretched and got his hat. We walked to the door and when he turned to face me, I knew he was going to kiss me. It was the gentlest and warmest kiss I've ever had. I felt myself melting and the kiss went down to my toes.

"I will call you tomorrow. I want to see you again."

All I wanted was another one of his kisses. "Me too. I had a wonderful time tonight and will talk to you tomorrow."

I watched Rex walk to his car and couldn't help wonder where this was all going. I quickly took off my clothes and put on a robe, washed my face and brushed my teeth before crawling between my freshly washed sheets. I slept better that night than I had in years. I dreamed of that sensuous kiss and Rex's arms around me.

# Chapter Four

It was eight in the morning when I woke up with my cat, Smokey, staring me in the face. "I assume you want your breakfast." I always talked to my cat as he had become my constant companion since my husband died. I got up, put on my robe from the night before and walked out to the kitchen. The coffee cups on the coffee table reminded me of sitting with Rex and talking until wee hours of the morning.

I fed Smokey and make a fresh pot of coffee. Just as I sat down with the morning paper, the phone rang.

"Good morning, Darl'n. Are you up?"

"Uh, yes. I was just having a cup of coffee. How about you?"

"I really didn't get much more than a nap when I got home. I came back to a mother cow getting ready to have her first calf and I sat up with her."

"Oh dear, is she okay?" I really knew nothing about cows, let alone how they gave birth.

"I am afraid she is going to have a difficult time with this calf. The calf isn't in the correct position for a normal delivery. The vet has been here for the past two hours. What I wanted to call you about is, first to let you know what a wonderful evening last night was and second that I will be tied up with this calf the rest of the day. I had hoped we could do something this evening, but I can't commit right now."

"I understand. Will you call me and let me know how the calf and the mother do?"

I hung up the phone disappointed. On the other hand, I was impressed at the considerate gesture of his phone call and that he did want to see me.

I spent the day doing yard work, not much because the Arizona summer sun is intense. I went to the gym and worked out for an hour, stopping at the grocery store on the way home. If all went well, I planned to ask Rex over for dinner and wanted to be prepared.

The day was coming to an end and I was out of chores. I did what I always do when I want to relax, I started composing music. I had a tune that kept going through my head since I first met Rex and needed to get it down on paper before it escaped me. I had the words and was working on the melody when the phone rang. It was eight o'clock. "Hey, how is it going, Darl'n?"

"I was writing a song and thinking about you. How is the calving going?"

"It was touch and go for a while, but the mother cow delivered a healthy male calf."

"I am glad to hear that. How are you doing?"

"To tell you the truth, I'm exhausted."

"Why don't you get some sleep and call me when you can. I miss you."

"I miss you too and sleep sounds wonderful. I'll call you when I get up."

I finished the melody to my song about midnight. I wondered when I'd hear from Rex.

# Chapter Five

I was in a deep sleep when the phone woke me up the following morning. I reached over to the bedside table and unplugged the charger. "Hello."

"Good morning, Darl'n. Are you awake?"

"Yep."

"You don't sound awake."

"Keep talking and I'll be fully awake."

"I have to come into town today and wondered if you'd like to come back with me. I'd like to show you the ranch and the new calf."

"I'd love to. What time are you coming?"

"I'm about twenty minutes from your front door."

Oh, my. Twenty minutes was not long to take a shower and get dressed.

"I'll leave the front door unlocked. Come in and have a cup of coffee if I'm not ready."

I jumped out of bed, unlocked the front door and ran through the shower. Knowing I would be outside, I put on light makeup, mascara and lipstick. My favorite blue jeans had been washed and were hanging in the closet. I slid into my jeans and put on a sleeveless t-shirt. Just as I was putting on my boots, I heard the front door open. There was my man, looking as handsome and yummy as he had the night before, minus the fancy clothes.

"I haven't made the coffee yet." I said coming out of the bedroom.

"Don't bother. We can get a cup to go in town. Are you ready?"

This man doesn't fool around. "Give me another minute to feed Smokey and I'll be ready to go."

"Don't forget your guitar. I want to hear your new song."

I grabbed my guitar and purse as we headed out the door.

"Good morning, Darl'n," Rex said as he opened the door for me to his truck and gave me a sweet good morning kiss.

"Coffee, I need coffee," I muttered crawling into the truck.

"There's a drive through Starbuck's down the street. It's an hour drive to the ranch, so you might want to get a large cup."

We got our coffee and drove east out of town.

"How many times do you make a trip into town?"

"A couple of times a week to get supplies for the ranch. I have a foreman who takes care of the supplies for the stock."

We talked on the way to the ranch. I learned that he had over 2,000 head of cattle.

"I inherited the ranch from my dad when he died fifteen years ago. I have one brother who didn't like ranching, so he got inheritance money and I got land and cattle."

"Sounds like a good deal to me. If you don't have any children, who gets the ranch when you die?"

"My brother has one son, my nephew Cole. He has loved the ranch ever since he was a little kid. He's my foreman now and will inherit what I have one day."

We came to a large stone arched driveway with a rod iron emblem on the top that said, Double R Ranch. "What does the Double R Ranch stand for?"

"My grandfather started the ranch back in the 1800's. His name was Robert and my grandmother's name was Rosie, so the "R" is for their first names."

We drove for another fifteen minutes in silence. I was admiring the land and pastures when Rex broke my trance.

"Here we are Darl'n." Rex made a sweeping turn into a circular gravel driveway. As we passed a grove of trees, the ranch house became visible.

"Oh, my! It certainly is beautiful here."

"It helps to have a gardener keep up the outside. I don't have the interest or time to do yard work. Come on in and let me show you around."

The house was a one-story ranch style home with a huge great room and a stone fireplace with western furniture. We walked into the dining room that had the same tasteful western décor. "I'm anxious to see the kitchen."

"The kitchen was remodeled a couple of years before my wife died."

I was in for a treat. There was a sub-zero refrigerator and all of the appliances were top of the line. "What a marvelous kitchen for entertaining. I love the island and eating bar."

The remainder of the tour was just as exciting. "I'll bet you have a maid."

"Yep, I like a clean and neat house but I am not going to do the work to keep it that way."

"May I ask how may square feet you have in the house?"

"It is just over 5,000 square feet."

"Impressive, but what I love most about it is how comfortable it feels."

We walked outside to a covered patio complete with a built in BBQ and smoker. "Do you like to cook outside?"

"We used to do a lot of entertaining before my wife died, but I haven't done much since then." I felt no reason to comment and we walked back into the house.

"When do I get to see the new calf?" I asked excitedly.

"That's where we're going right now."

The barn was as immaculate as the house. Lucky cows.

Before we got to the stall where the calf was housed with its mother, I noticed a good- looking young man of about thirty years. "Roxie, this is my nephew, Cole. He lives here with me and is my foreman."

Cole shook my hand and I couldn't help but notice he had the same steel blue eyes as Rex.

"Let's go see that calf. How's he doing, Cole?"

"There are no problems and we'll be able to turn him and his mom out soon."

"Here's the little guy," Rex said as he opened the stall door.

The calf was feeding from his mom and looked up as we entered the stall.

"Oh, my! He is cute. May I pet him?"

"Of course."

I sat down on the hay next to the calf and gently stroked his newborn hide. I could have stayed there all day, but Rex motioned it was time to go. "There's lots more I want to show you."

We walked back to the house and Rex grabbed a couple of water bottles. It was then that I noticed a framed photo of Rex and a very pretty woman. "Is this you and your wife?"

"Yes, that one was taken a year before she died."

Rex handed me the water bottles and we walked out to the truck.

"Where are we going?"

"That's a surprise." I loved surprises and told Rex so.

We drove about a quarter of a mile before I saw any cattle. "We keep the stock away from the house to reduce the manure smell and keep the flies away."

"How do you keep track of so many cows?"

"They are called cattle, Darl'n. Their ears are tagged and we contain them with fences around the property. Every now and then one gets out and we have to round them up."

It was then that I noticed a cowboy on a horse. "Do you still cowboy on a horse?"

"Yep. Lots of ranchers are using ATVs to round up cattle, but we prefer horses. It's less stressful for the cattle."

We had driven another half mile or so when I saw a stream and a grove of trees. "If you look hard enough, there's a small cabin in that grove."

"How adorable, but does anyone live there?"

"Not now. It was the first house my grandparents built when they started the ranch. I keep it up now thinking Cole will get married one day and have kids. It would be a great place for sleepovers."

"Let's stop. I'd like to see the inside."

Rex parked the truck and took my hand as we walked to the front of the cabin. This was the first time he held my hand and I loved the warmth and strength of his fingers entwined in mine.

The cabin had three bedrooms, living room, dining room and kitchen. The kitchen appliances had been upgraded, but not as fine as the ranch house. "Is there a bathroom?" I asked because I was curious and also because my bladder was about to burst.

"The outhouse is outside," Rex told me with a straight face.

"What?" I would rather find a large tree than use an outhouse.

"I was kidding. The bathroom is off the first bedroom. It was added on after the house was built."

"I will be right back."

"See you at the truck."

It was noon when we took off in the truck again. "I'm getting hungry. I'll bet you had no breakfast," he turned to me as he drove.

"I could use a little nourishment. That coffee only woke me up."

"There is a small town about twenty miles from here. It has a little café that used to be the train depot. The food is pretty good."

"Sounds great."

The café was packed when we arrived. We were seated and Rex seemed to know everyone in the place, including the waitresses. The menu looked fabulous. I expected hamburgers and fries but found vegan choices, salads and wonderful sounding sandwiches. I ordered a salad and Rex had the BBQ plate. Several folks stopped by the table and Rex introduced me, each time he proudly put his arm around me.

When we got back to the ranch house, Rex told me he had some chores to do. I could either go with him, or relax in the house. I opted to stay at the house.

"Good, you can see what is in the refrigerator for dinner tonight."

"Who is cooking?" I asked laughing.

"You are, of course."

"You got it." I remembered that I told Rex I loved to cook the first night we met and he was going to take me up on it.

I puttered around in the kitchen looking into cabinets and seeing what staples he had for cooking. The cabinets were fully stocked as was the refrigerator. I peeked into the freezer and found beef, chicken, seafood and hotdogs.

The hot dogs are out. I was making a mental list of recipes I loved and could cook from memory. One that stood out was a pasta primavera with scallops. Oops, there are no scallops, but there is shrimp. Just as good.

I found all of the ingredients I would need with the exception of white wine. There was one pantry I had not explored yet and when I opened the door, I found a wine cellar. Is there nothing this man doesn't have?

I started thawing the shrimp and realized the white wine didn't need to go into the refrigerator because it was already the perfect temperature in the wine cellar. Now to find the dishes and placemats. I found them in the Chinese cabinet in the dining room. Even though it was mid-afternoon, I set the table.

With dinner preparations underway, I went into the great room. There were more pictures of Rex and his wife. They looked like a lovely couple. I wondered if they were as happy as they looked. The couch was too inviting not to sit on. I snuggled up in the overstuffed leather cushions, put my head down and promptly went to sleep.

I was awakened with a soft, tender kiss. At first, I thought I was dreaming but when I opened my eyes, Rex was leaning over me. He had an incredible smile.

"I guess I fell asleep."

"I guess you did. Go back to sleep for a little while. I am going to take a quick shower and change clothes."

I complied with his suggestion thinking how comfortable I was with Rex.

Rex woke me up again twenty minutes later. "It's four o'clock and it's happy hour. What would you like to drink?"

"Hmmm, I'm not sure. What would you suggest?"

"Why don't you go out on the patio and I'll surprise you."

"Another surprise?" I said as I got up and headed to the patio.

It was starting to cool off and the patio was a perfect spot for relaxing. Rex came out within minutes with a bottle of Cabernet Sauvignon, wine glasses and a plate of fruit, crackers and cheese.

Rex motioned to a lounge chair made for two. "Wouldn't you rather sit with me?" I needed no further encouragement. We sat down, Rex opened the wine and we snuggled back into the cushions with our drinks. He put his arm around me and I put my head on his shoulder. We stayed like that, sipping wine and munching on cheese, until the sun started to go down.

"It doesn't get any better than this," he whispered kissing me softly on the ear.

"No, it doesn't," I said as I snuggled closer.

"What are we having for dinner?" Rex asked.

"Pasta primavera."

"That sounds fantastic. Can I help with the cooking?"

"Nope and as much as I'd like to stay here, I should start dinner."

"Is it okay if I watch?"

"I would be disappointed if you didn't."

Dinner turned out as scrumptious as I had hoped. We dined, drank white wine and talked for two hours. He asked me more about my music. It was getting late and I was thinking about the hour drive home.

"I really need to get going. Let me do the dishes and you can drive me home."

"Leave the dishes and the maid can clean up tomorrow. Come on, you are tired and I have two hours of driving."

I was pleased that Rex didn't suggest I spend the night. Picking up my guitar, I realized I hadn't played for him. I didn't say anything and neither did Rex. I could always play another day.

It was midnight when Rex dropped me off at the house. As I unlocked the door, he put his hand over my head and rested it on the door jam. "Darl'n this was a wonderful day. Can I see you again soon?"

"As soon as you can get back this way." I stood on my tip toes, put my arms around his neck and gave him a long, passionate kiss. He encircled my body with his strong arms and kissed me back.

"I'll call you tomorrow."

I was exhausted, but high on feelings for this man. I found Smokey and we curled up on the couch and fell asleep. An hour later, my cell phone rang. I jumped up off the couch, waking Smokey who meowed and I located the phone in my purse.

"Hello."

"I just got home and wanted to tell you I miss you."

I was suddenly awake. Looking at the clock, it was one o'clock in the morning.

"Are you OK?" I asked.

"Just missing you. Go back to sleep and I'll talk to you later."

Smokey and I crawled into bed and I slept soundly for the remainder of the night.

# Chapter Six

It is a good thing I am retired because this man, who requires no sleep, called me at six in the morning.

"Did I wake you up?"

"Of course not, I was awake and waiting for your call."

"Darl'n, you were asleep. Now to get on with the day's activities. I need to buy a new bull at the auction today. Are you up for this?"

Why can't he buy a bull at a reasonable time of the day? "Of course, I am up for buying a bull. When should I be ready to go?"

Come to find out, Rex was half way to my house when he called. That meant I had thirty minutes to shower and get dressed. I am going to become a marathon dresser I thought.

Rex arrived looking like he never needed a night's sleep. Damn that man, doesn't he ever sleep?

The auction was ten miles out of town. "Let's get some breakfast in town before we head out."

"How about I fix an omelet at the house. Then we can have coffee while I'm cooking breakfast."

"That's sounds great. I can do the coffee while you do the eggs."

Breakfast was one of my best. "That was delicious. I am going to have to have you around to cook for me all of the time," Rex exclaimed.

We put the dishes in the dish washer and headed out. The drive to the auction was over a well-used dirt road full of pot holes. "Does anyone maintain this road?" I asked as I was tossed about the cab of the truck.

"Not really, but they have the best stock for sale and at the best prices."

Once we got to the auction grounds, we got out and signed up for an auction number. Rex didn't bid until an enormous bull was presented for auction. "The bid starts at $3,000." The auctioneer announced. The bid was up to $5,000 and Rex was still silent. I knew to remain quiet as he concentrated on the bid.

When Rex bid $7,000 I couldn't' believe it. That was a lot of money for a cow, okay a bull.

"What else are you going to buy today?" I inquired.

"I only wanted that bull. Even at the price I paid, it's a bargain considering the calves hell sire."

So, I learned another thing about ranching. Bulls were expensive but very valuable.

"Are we taking the bull home with us?"

"No, Darl'n. The bull will be delivered to the ranch in a couple of days."

We left the auction grounds around noon. "I have a great place for a picnic. Are you hungry?"

"You should know after being dragged from my bed and a sound sleep that I am hungry by noon."

"What do you mean dragged from your bed? It was just after six in the morning when I called."

"Exactly what I mean," as I gave him a gentle shove on the arm. "Besides, we don't have any food for a picnic."

"Ah, guess again my pet." That was the first time he called me anything other than Darl'n.

"Ok, I am game. Where are we going?"

When there was no response, I said, "I know, it's a surprise."

"How did you know?"

# Chapter Seven

Rex headed back to the ranch and when he got to a large oak tree he pulled the truck over and parked. "This tree has been here since my grandparents homesteaded." The tree was gorgeous with heavy branches extending to the ground. As I explored the area, Rex took out a blanket and picnic basket from the back of the truck.

"Now, I can't take credit for this lunch. The maid, Lupe, fixed us something before I left this morning. I told her I needed something 'especial' for my new friend."

"I see, and did you tell her who I was?"

"Of course. I told her you were the woman who stole my heart."

I was moved by his comment. I sat on the picnic blanket and pulled him to the ground. "That kind of comment will get you in trouble."

"Yeah, and just what do you have in mind?"

Rex was lying on the blanket in seconds. We embraced and kissed. "Do you know that you are incredible?" he asked.

"I hope so."

The next hour was beyond words. The sky was blue and the sounds of nature filled the air. I couldn't have been happier. Toward the late afternoon, we both had fallen asleep in each other's arms. I woke up first and gazed at this man I knew I was falling in love with. Rex made these wonderful waking up noises, looked up at me and gave me a hug.

"I think we fell asleep. Did we eat lunch?" He asked.

"I don't believe we did. Are you hungry?"

"No, but it's getting late and we should be getting back."

We picked up the blanket and folded it. Rex got the picnic basket that we never opened and we headed for the truck.

The sky had turned a dark color and looked like rain. By the time we got back to the ranch, the rain had started.

"How about you stay at the ranch tonight. Rains in Arizona can turn into floods quickly and I can't leave the cattle."

I didn't have any extra clothes, but I knew Rex wouldn't ask me to stay if it wasn't necessary. I didn't know if he was asking me to sleep in his bed.

Reading my mind, he said, "There's an extra bedroom you can use. Chances are I won't get much sleep tonight."

# Chapter Eight

I slept in fits of dreams while the rains continued and the thunder and lightning filled the skies. I woke up at three in the morning, put on one of Rex's shirts from the closet and wandered out to the kitchen. Rex was just finishing a cup of coffee. He and Cole were talking about going out to check on the cattle.

"The danger with the cattle is that they can get caught in a flash flood, or drown in the rising waters from the creek," Rex was saying. He looked up and saw me standing in the doorway of the kitchen.

"Can't sleep?"

"The thunder woke me up. Are you going out in the storm?"

"We don't have a choice, Darl'n. If we can save some of the cattle it's a plus for the ranch."

"What can I do to help?"

"Are you serious?"

"Of course," I responded.

I quickly got dressed and the three of us headed back to the truck. We drove through rain, puddles and streams of water. "Rex, look over there," Cole yelled. "There's a cow stuck in the water and mud."

Rex turned the truck around and I could see the cow struggling against the onslaught of water. Rex and Cole jumped out of the truck and ran to the cow. They started tugging on her head trying to free her from the water and muck. When it appeared to be useless, the cow let out a loud moo and she was pulled free.

We jumped back into the truck and started driving. I had begun to wonder why I agreed to come with Rex and Cole. What could I do? I certainly couldn't pull cows out of the water. We hadn't gone far when Rex stopped the truck. "We need to get the cattle out of the arroyo before the flash floods come," he said to Cole. The men got out of the truck and started to round up the cattle on foot. Without a task to do, I wandered off to the arroyo, then free of water.

"Roxie, get back," I heard Rex scream. I looked up and saw a wall of water coming towards me. As I turned to run, I tripped on a rock, fell and hit my head. That was the last I remembered. I lay there unconscious until Rex rescued me and I woke up in the hospital two days later.

"What happened," I asked, looking at Rex who hadn't shaved in days.

"You almost got washed away in an arroyo and I nearly lost you."

The nurse came in the room. "Sweetie, your fellow has not left your bedside since you came in."

"How long has that been?"

"Two days."

"What about Smokey. He needs to eat and be taken care of."

"Cole went to your house and brought Smokey back to the ranch. He's fine."

"How did you get in without a key?"

"Well, let's just say that there are ways."

Reassured Smokey was okay, I closed my eyes and went to sleep. Shortly, I knew Rex had crawled in bed with me and snuggled against my body, his arm across my chest. I knew I was safe.

# Chapter Nine

The next day I was discharged from the hospital. "I'm going to take you back to the ranch for a couple of days. The doctor said someone needs to watch over you."

I was in no place to argue with Rex. With Smokey at the ranch, there was no reason to go home. Within two blocks of the hospital, I started to vomit. Not just a little bit, but gastronomical heaves from my stomach. I heard Rex calling the hospital.

"Darl'n, there has been a change of plans. We are going to your place. The doctor said to watch you and if the vomiting persists, we need to go back to the hospital."

"Can Cole bring Smokey back to the house?"

"Of course, I will call him right now."

I vomited once more after I got home and then was ravenously hungry. All Rex would give me was soda crackers and hot tea. "I want a hamburger," I demanded. Rex informed me in no uncertain terms that was to going to happen. Through my hunger, I loved him for taking care of me.

Cole brought Smokey home that evening. He immediately crawled in bed with me and we went to sleep.

The next morning, I woke up at five o'clock. Now what is that all about? I thought looking at the clock. I got up and put on my robe. My goodness, now Rex knows I don't sleep in pajamas because I wasn't wearing any and didn't have any in my closet. When I went to the great room, I saw Rex asleep on the couch. I knelt down beside him and nuzzled his neck. He woke up, looked at me and in an instant, I was in his arms.

"Darl'n, how are you?"

"I am hungrier than a bear and want more than crackers and tea for breakfast."

"Then I shall fix you breakfast if you will get off my chest."

We both laughed. I released him from my chest hold and we went to the kitchen where he prepared a breakfast of eggs, hash browns, toast and coffee. I was a happy woman.

# Chapter Ten

Rex stayed with me until early that afternoon when he was satisfied, I would be okay. "I need to get back to the ranch and relieve Cole. I don't think he's gotten much sleep these past few days." The rains were over, but the cattle were spread out over the ranch and needed to be accounted for.

"Do you have anyone to help you?"

"We have several ranch hands that we've called in to help with the cattle."

"Call me when you get home."

"You know I will." Rex took me in his arms and gave me a hug and a long, warm kiss before he left.

I took a hot shower thinking how wonderful the past two weeks had been. Rex and I had been together most of these days and I knew it was taking a toll on him being away from the ranch for so long. On the other hand, he had Cole to take charge. Just as I got out of the shower, Rex called.

"There is more damage than I thought," he started. "The road to the house is washed out and the creek is still running high. I think we have accounted for most of the cattle and only lost a dozen or so in the floods."

Before I could say anything, he told me he had to go and would call later. "I miss you," was the last thing he said before he hung up.

The rest of the day was filled with laundry and minor chores

We Fell In Love

around the house. As I picked up my guitar, the doorbell rang. Now who is that? I don't know anyone that would come unannounced.

Smokey beat me to the door, always the curious cat. When I opened the door, I was face to face with a huge bouquet of red roses. "Oh my," was all I could say. I accepted the flowers and found a card hidden inside the bouquet. Of course, they were from Rex. When did he find the time to send me flowers? The card read, 'I will pick you up in the morning at eight o'clock. Bring your work boots and an overnight bag. Don't forget your guitar and Smokey.'

I was speechless which was good because I had no one to talk to other than Smokey. I immediately found my phone and sent him a text, 'The roses are beautiful. I will be ready at eight. I miss you.'

I picked up Smokey and danced around the room. "Come on Smokey we have things to do and you have to pack your kitty overnight bag." Smokey meowed and jumped out of my arms. "Silly cat."

Without more information I assumed I would be helping around the ranch. I didn't have any work clothes, or work boots so I picked out the oldest clothes and boots I had and threw in a couple of nice outfits for the evening. When I finished laying out my clothes on the bed, I needed more than an overnight bag. Oh well, I thought as I pulled out my suitcase from under the bed.

I was up early the next morning and ready when Rex rang the doorbell. When he saw my suitcase, guitar and vase of roses, he laughed and asked if I was going on a trip. "A girl can never be too ready," I said as we hugged and kissed.

Driving to the ranch, I asked "What kind of work do you have lined up for me?"

"One thing for sure, I want you to stay away from the water. You scared me to death when I saw you standing in front of the oncoming flash flood. Have you ever seen a flash flood before?"

"No, but I've heard of them. I didn't realize they could move so fast."

43

"Darl'n, I'm not sure what I would have done if something had happened to you."

That was about the sweetest thing any guy had ever told me. I didn't know what to say and reached over and squeezed his arm.

As we approached the ranch house, I could see the damage the rains and flood had done. The road had been cleared but there were gullies and holes along the side.

"WOW, things are a mess."

"Yep. Cole and I only had time to deal with the cattle. Now we need to take an inventory of the land and house and see what needs to be repaired."

"What can I do to help?"

"Having you here is the biggest help."

Just then we turned into the driveway. Rex collected my things from the truck. As I stepped into a mud puddle, I was glad I had on old clothes and boots.. I picked up Smokey and let him down in the house.

"I am going back to help Cole. Make yourself at home and we'll be back for lunch."

I wasn't sure what I would do the rest of the morning. The house was big and there were rooms I hadn't explored. "Come on Smokey, let's take a look around." There were a total of five bedrooms and bathrooms. My goodness, this must take a week to clean. I deduced that Cole had the room in the back since there were jeans and muddy boots on the floor. With Rex in the master bedroom, that left three bedrooms. I found the room I slept in the night of the storm. I brought my suitcase back, but didn't unpack it. The last two bedrooms were tastefully decorated in western motif and didn't look like they had been used.

"Okay, Smokey, let's go see what I can rustle up for lunch." I wanted to serve lunch outside, but the temperature was in the nineties, so I settled for the island counter. Looking in the refrigerator, I found fixings for a salad and sandwiches, not very exciting, but it was hot outside and I knew the sandwiches would be filling for my hungry men.

With lunch prepared and the counter top set, I decided to see the rest of the house. "Come on Smokey." There was one room I hadn't noticed before off the great room. The door was open. I flipped on the light and walked into a magnificent office. This is definitely Rex's domain with the manly furniture and western paintings on the wall. As I walked around the room, I identified a Remington bronze statue of a cowboy on a horse. That must have cost a couple of bucks. The massive wood desk had papers neatly stacked. It was then that I noticed the framed photographs on the wall above the fireplace. As I got closer, I could see they were rodeo pictures. I identified a young Rex on a horse during a tie-down roping event. The next picture was of Rex on a bucking bronco, one hand in the air and the other on the rope reins. I could envision the bronc bucking as the crowd cheered. Just then, I heard male voices in the kitchen. "Come on Smokey, let's go feed those hungry cowboys."

# Chapter Eleven

Rex and Cole talked about the damage they found and made a list of work that needed to be done. They finished lunch and left for the afternoon.

After cleaning up the kitchen, I laid down on the sofa and fell fast asleep. I was dreaming that I was floating on a cloud and being tucked into its fluffy layers. When I woke up, I was in bed and under the covers. Rex was sleeping in the chair next to me. He woke up when I turned over.

"How did I get here?" I asked.

Being somewhat of a rhetorical question, Rex smiled and closed his eyes. It was six o'clock by the clock on the bedside stand. I got up, went to the bathroom and splashed cold water on my face.

"I was worried about you. The doctor said that you had a nasty hit on the head and to make sure you didn't get so drowsy I couldn't wake you up for the next 72 hours."

When I turned around, Rex was standing behind me. I was in his arms in seconds feeling his body warmth from his nap.

"Do you think you are up for dinner? I am starved," he said releasing me from his hold.

"I thawed out some steaks after lunch. How does that sound?"

"Fantastic. While you are fixing dinner, I'll clean off the grill."

When Rex returned from the patio, he left to take a shower and clean up. I knew he had returned by his fresh smell. That and the fact he hugged me from behind and gave me a kiss on the neck. "You don't know how wonderful it is to have you here on the ranch."

I turned around to face him. "I love being here," and laid my head on his chest. "I just opened a bottle of red wine. Would you like a glass?" I asked as I raised my head.

"I'll pour and start the fire when you are ready."

Rex sat down at the island counter and watched me as I finished the preparations for dinner. He started the fire and offered to cook the steaks. I was only too happy to have him part of making our meal. I set the table in the dining room and found some candles for a little ambiance.

"That was one of the best meals I've had a long time." Rex commented after we finished our dinner.

"You have a maid, do you have a cook?"

"No, I'm not home enough to have someone come in and cook meals."

"You have a refrigerator full of food. Who eats it?"

"Cole often brings his girlfriend over for the evening, and I suspect for the night. They stock the refrigerator in the event their friends come over."

"Why haven't I seen Cole or his girlfriend while I have been here?"

"He's staying in the cabin to give us some private time."

We finished the last of the wine. "Leave the dishes and let's go into the great room. I want to hear your new song."

I was delighted by his request and took my guitar out of its case. I spent a few minutes tuning it and going over the words in my head. I closed my eyes and began strumming the strings of the guitar and singing with all my heart.

*I have searched for love,*
*Floating on a morning dove.*
*I have longed for romance,*
*Swaying like an exotic dance.*

47

*Two people coming together,*
*Floating high light as a feather.*
*Love and devotion will be ours,*
*Reaching high to the shooting stars.*

With my last strum, I looked over at Rex and his eyes were closed. "Did you know you have the most beautiful voice?"

"Thank you."

"Love and devotion . . . I like that." He closed his eyes again and was soon asleep.

I took the opportunity to tip toe to my bedroom and unpack my suitcase. Humming my new song, I laid out my clothes wondering how many days I would be staying. Smokey was asleep on the bed. It looks like Smokey is comfortable and making himself at home I thought. I chuckled to myself watching his furry body rise with his sleepy respirations.

I undressed and laid in the big king-sized bed under exquisitely smooth sheets wondering just how long we would be sleeping in separate beds. I was sure I was in love with Rex and felt he had the same feelings for me. The last time I looked at the clock it was one in the morning. It was also the last time I slept by myself.

"I can't wait any longer to make love to you," were the soft words I heard in my ear. Rex was under the covers next to my body before I was fully aware of what was happening.

"You really don't sleep in pajamas, do you?"

"No, and it appears that you don't either," I replied giggling.

"Roxie, I love you and want you so badly I ache. I need to know how you feel before anything happens tonight."

"Sweetheart, I have been in love with you from the first night we met. I didn't want to admit it to myself until just recently. When I went to bed tonight, I wondered how long we would be in separate bedrooms."

Rex kissed me and we made passionate and wonderful love. I

couldn't help thinking how love and sharing two bodies is different when we get older as to the hyped up hormone driven love in our early years.

I whispered "I love you," in Rex's ear as he fell asleep after we made love for the second time. I was soon asleep in his arms.

The sun woke us up at six o'clock. Rex rolled over and gave me a kiss. "Come on sleepy head, we are going horseback riding today."

"We're doing what?"

"Riding horses. You do ride, don't you?"

"Uh, not really. I've done a little trail riding on some very tame and slow horses."

"Then you shall learn to ride properly."

"OK, would you like to shower first?"

"Oh no you don't. I'd like nothing better than taking a shower with you and covering your body with sudsy soap."

Giggling, I jumped out of bed with Rex behind me. Fifteen minutes later, we emerged from the steamy shower. Grabbing big fluffy white towels, we dried each other off.

"After we get dressed, I'll get the horses ready while you fix us breakfast. You might also fix a lunch to take, we may be out for several hours."

I dried my hair, put on a little make-up all the while smiling and humming my new song. It was going to be another hot day, so I opted for a sleeveless t-shirt and cover up shirt to prevent sunburn.

"You look like a young bride," Rex said as he came into the kitchen and giving me a kiss on the back of my neck.

Blushing, I said, "Young I feel, I don't know about the bride part."

Rex grabbed a cup of coffee and headed out to the barn smiling. If I listened carefully, I could hear him humming my song.

# Chapter Twelve

Rex had two beautiful horses waiting. I didn't know what kind of horses they were, only that they were big.

"Which one is mine?"

"I would think the smaller of the two. This is Lady. She is a five-year old quarter horse and very gentle."

"And who is the bigger horse?"

"This is Honey, a Palomino and one of my favorite riding horses. Okay, let's get started on a few pointers." Rex took me by the shoulders and turned me to face Lady. "This is the front and the back of the horse, "he said pointing to Lady. I looked at him and rolled my eyes.

"Do you know which side of the horse to mount?"

"I assume either side."

"No, you mount the horse from the left side. Forget all of those cowboy movies where cowboys jump onto the saddle. The easiest way to get onto the saddle is with a mounting block. Any solid elevated surface will do."

"Like that block over there?"

"Yep, that is a mounting block. But before you actually get on the horse, especially one that is not familiar to you, it is important to develop rapport with the animal."

"Like petting and talking to the horse."

"You got it. Lady knows you are here and is curious about who you are. See she keeps turning her head around. Now it's your turn to go to the front of the horse and introduce yourself."

Not knowing what I was doing, I walked up to Lady's head, petted her on the neck and began to talk to her. I told her who I was and that I was going to ride her today and hoped she would be easy on me.

"See how she shakes her head up and down. That means she knows what you're going to do. Maybe not in English, but by the tone of your voice. Are you ready to get on Lady?"

I walked to the mounting block and Rex brought Lady to me. "Now take the reins in your left hand and hold them without too much tension. Grab hold of Lady's mane. Don't worry, you won't hurt her. Now put your left foot in the stirrup and swing your right leg over."

I followed Rex's detailed instructions and found I was sitting in the saddle on Lady's back. Rex congratulated me on my accomplishment and he went to mount Honey. OK, I am sitting on a horse, now what do I do?

How to Ride a Horse 101 was easy with Rex. He was patient and started with how to gently kick the horse to get it to move. Then he went over how to pull on the reins to get the horse to go left or right. Once I had this down, he was ready to hit the trail. "Just follow me and remember what I told you."

We started out with a slow walk. It was a beautiful day and I was thinking that riding a horse is not such a big deal. Then Rex went down a rocky slope. Lady followed and suddenly I was being rocked in all directions in the saddle. I heard Rex yell, "Lean back in the saddle." I obeyed his command and found the rocking wasn't as bad.

The morning went quickly. We stopped around noon for lunch. Rex helped me off of Lady. When my feet hit the ground, my legs and knees buckled. He grabbed me before I fell on my butt. "Until you get used to riding, those inner thigh muscles get a work out. Let's take a break and eat lunch."

Rex brought out a blanket and got our lunch from his saddle

bags. "Why is this heavy?" He asked carrying the bag to the blanket.

"I put in a bottle of wine."

"That's my girl."

I took the sandwiches out of the bag and gave one to Rex. "What is this? Peanut Butter and Jelly?"

"Yeah, but it is the best P&J you'll ever have."

I wasn't in a hurry to get back on Lady. We lazed in the sun and I asked him about the rodeo photographs over the fireplace in his office.

"I keep those as a reminder."

"What do you mean?"

"I was very young, in my late teens, and I told my parents I was going to do the rodeo circuit riding broncos and team roping. They were against me going and I essentially left home to compete in the rodeos. I was actually pretty good and had a great time for the first two years. Then in my third year, I was thrown from a bronc and broke my back."

I was listening intently and didn't want to interrupt his story.

"I was air lifted to a major trauma hospital and admitted to the intensive care unit. My parents were there within hours. The doctor wanted to take me to the operating room and insert rods to stabilize my back. I had the surgery and then spent a month in the hospital and another six months in physical therapy. It took a long time for me to get back on a horse."

"That explains the scar down your back."

"I came back to the ranch when I got out of the hospital and learned ranching from my dad. I've lived here all of my life and will no doubt die here. That reminds me, Cole is bringing his girlfriend over for dinner tonight. I hope you don't mind playing hostess and chef."

"I'd love to meet his girlfriend. What is her name? And no, I don't mind being hostess and chef."

'Her name is Angelina. She's a beautiful young lady and comes from Spanish descent. Her ancestors settled in the United States many years ago and own a large ranch. If she and Cole get married, they will have more acreage than they know what to do with."

Rex was ready to leave. "Come on Darl'n, let me help you get up on Lady."

# Chapter Thirteen

I was glad I packed some evening clothes considering we were entertaining for the first time. Rex was busy in his office and I set about preparing dinner. I thought about a Mexican menu, but then remembered that Angelina was Spanish and I didn't want to compete with her culinary background. We didn't get back from horseback riding until four o'clock, so there wasn't a lot of time. Filet Mignon wrapped in bacon on the grill sounded good and easy with twice baked potatoes and a salad. Oh lah! Dinner was planned and in the works.

I was in the master bathroom getting dressed after a quick shower when Rex came in and gave me a bear hug. "Have I told you how much I love you?"

"Hmm, I think I remember something like that. Cole and Angelina are due in twenty minutes. Get a move on." I affectionately patted his butt.

"Yes, Mam. I will see you in ten minutes."

Twenty minutes later Cole and Angelina arrived. Rex was correct, she was a beautiful woman with dark eyes and dark hair. She wore tight jeans with a light blue shirt that set off her dark features. Cole introduced us just as Rex was coming out of the bedroom looking his scrumptious self. Angelina offered to help with dinner and the men went into the office to do whatever men do together.

"Cole tells me that you are the love of Rex's life. That is so wonderful. He has been alone for too long."

"We've both alone for too long," I replied.

We worked in tandem fixing dinner. Angelina needed no direction in setting the table and I found her to be delightful. The four of us ate dinner and drank two bottles of exceptional red wine from the wine cellar.

"Roxie, would you play for us?" Rex requested.

"What do you play?" Angelina asked.

Rex interjected, "You should hear her play the guitar. She also plays the piano."

I took several requests, most of which I knew. I was completely taken by surprise when Angelina asked if she could play my guitar. What a treat to hear her play and sing songs in her first language. It was as if a song bird had flown into the room.

I looked at the clock as it struck midnight. Rex and I had a long day riding in the sun. We were both tired and Cole and Angelina picked up on it. They suggested it was time for them to leave and we didn't try to get them to stay longer.

"Darl'n, I am tired, how about you?"

"My bed or yours?" I asked with a mischievous grin.

"How about we sleep in my room from now on. Grab your toothbrush and we can move your clothes tomorrow."

# Chapter Fourteen

Rex had chores to do during the day. Sometimes I went with him and other times I stayed at the house. I had been at the ranch for over ten days and felt a need to go home and regroup. When I told Rex I needed some time at my house, he understood. During the hour drive, I felt I was leaving the ranch, my new home. I left Smokey at the ranch because he was settled and had enough changes in the past few weeks.

After Rex dropped me off, I wandered around lost. I didn't hear the sound of tractor noise or the whinny of horses. All I heard was silence interrupted by the intermittent passage of cars. I came to a decision and called Rex. "Sweetheart, I need to come back to the ranch with you. Have you headed back yet?"

"No, is everything okay?"

"Yes, it is just that I don't want to be in this house alone without you."

"I am out doing some business for the ranch. Can I pick you up in a couple of hours?"

"I was thinking I could follow you back in my car."

"That's a good idea, Darl'n. I will see you shortly."

I ran around like a mad lady and collected what I thought I needed at the ranch. Let's see. I need my computer. I can use Rex's printer. I need more changes of clothes. Books, I need books to read ... and so the thoughts ran through my head. Oh yes, I need to stop the newspaper and forward my mail. At the last minute I packed my guns with the thought I could practice shooting at the ranch.

I wondered what Rex would think when he arrived and saw all of my personal belongings stacked by the front door. I didn't have long to wait before Rex walked through the door. My heart leaped with love for him.

"Are you all set?" he asked smiling without making a comment on how many suitcases or boxes I had.

On the way to the ranch, I thought how far I had come since we met. I fought a monsoon flood; fell and got a concussion and was in the hospital; learned to ride a horse; and fell in love. The last part was the best part.

When we got home, Rex took my luggage and boxes into the house and went to find Cole. It was then that I noticed all of the pictures of his deceased wife had been taken down or removed.

Later that night at dinner, I asked him why he took the pictures down. He simply replied that it was time and the subject never came up again.

# Chapter Fifteen

I didn't know life could be so tranquil. We had survived the monsoon season and Rex, Cole and the ranch hands carried out what needed to be done to run a ranch.

"Darl'n, how would you like to plan a party? I usually throw a BBQ extravaganza on Labor Day and invite the neighbors and friends."

"I love planning parties. How many guests do you usually have?"

"Around two hundred."

"Two hundred!"

"We could invite more if you like."

"No, that's okay. I've never done a party that large before."

"Why don't you ask Angelina to help you? She's been involved in the event for the past couple of years."

"Sweetheart that is a great idea. I'll call her today."

Angelina was delighted to be part of the planning committee of two. We made a guest list, addressed the invitations, planned the menu, and talked about hiring a band and a catering company to provide and cook the food.

Angelina and Cole were often at the house for dinner. When we had our party plans together, we presented them to our men. The only suggestion they had was to tell the gardener to spruce up the grounds.

The more I was around Angelina, the more she was like the daughter I never had. I wondered if she and Cole would marry.

# We Fell In Love

The weeks flew by. I couldn't imagine not living with Rex on the ranch. I had always been a big city girl and wasn't interested in living in the country. Now I couldn't imagine going back to the city.

# Chapter Sixteen

It was a month before the party. I had driven back into town to Sissy's to buy a new outfit. On the way home, I stopped at the house. It seemed so sad with no one living in it. It brought back memories of when my late husband and I built our home. I wiped away a tear and remembered another phase of my life had started with Rex. I closed and locked the door.

When I arrived at the ranch, I noticed the vet's truck was there. Rex came out to the car. "Roxie, Smokey is sick. The vet is with him now."

We walked into the house. Smokey was listless and barely breathing.

"Roxie, I need to put Smokey down. He's dying and suffering."

"What's wrong with him?"

"Just old age. How old is he?"

"He's sixteen years old."

I cried on Rex's shoulder and then held Smokey for the last time. Rex dug a grave behind the house and we buried Smokey. I missed Smokey and spent my days mopping around the house. One day Rex came in with a big grin on his face.

"Darl'n, come with me."

"Where are we going?"

"Never mind, just come along."

When we got to the barn, Rex said, "You know those two barn

cats we have? Well, one of them has had a litter of kittens. Take a look."

I looked in the corner and on a bundle of straw I saw the mama cat and four kittens. "Oh my," was all I could say.

"We can't take them away from their mother yet, but why don't you pick one out and she can live in the house with us."

I visited the kittens each day and watched them grow stronger. One day, I decided I wanted two of the kittens. They would be great playmates having been litter mates. They had tuxedo coat markings and had to be twins. When I told Rex I wanted more than one of the kittens, he laughed and told me I could have all of them if I wanted. I named them Smokey II after my first Smokey and Tammy. I couldn't wait until they were six weeks old and could be weaned from their mother.

# Chapter Seventeen

As the party grew closer, Angelina and I spent more time together making sure all of the last-minute details were covered. One night at dinner, we went over the party plans with Rex and Cole. "I think you girls have it covered," Rex commented.

Cole asked how many people had RSVP'd. We looked at our list and reported that of the two hundred invitees, only ten couples had declined. That meant we had one hundred and eighty guests to feed.

The day of the party was hectic. The catering service arrived three hours early to set up their BBQ grills, assemble tables and chairs and the bar. We hired a band and the quartet arrived an hour before the guests. At Rex's suggestion, we hired a clown to keep the kids entertained.

At two o'clock the first guests started arriving. Appetizers were on the tables, the bar was open, meat was being grilled and the aroma was mouthwatering. Cars were being parked by the ranch hands. And the kids were entertained.

Rex introduced me to so many people that their names soon became a blur. He kept me by his side and was so proud. "Darl'n, you did a fantastic job and you look beautiful tonight," he whispered in my ear. I leaned up and kissed him, "Thank you on both compliments."

Two hours into the party, Cole was on stage with the microphone and was calling for everyone's attention. Angelina was at his side.

"Good afternoon and welcome to the Double R annual barbeque. We have Roxie and Angelina to thank for the coordination of this wonderful party." There was a round of applause which caused me to blush.

He took Angelina's hand, got down on one knee and looked up at her with love. "Angelina, I love you so much and want you to be my wife. Will you marry me? The crowd was delighted. Angelina replied in a sweet voice, "Yes Cole, I will marry you." With that Cole placed an engagement ring on her hand. The band started up, the crowd applauded and Cole gave out a loud yeehaw.

"That was so sweet, did you know about this?" I asked Rex.

"No. I am surprised as you are. I will say though that I've expected this for some time."

We wound our way through the crowd of people to Cole and Angelina. I gave Angelina a big hug, then Cole. Their announcement was the crowning glory to the party.

By eight o'clock the party was winding down, guests were leaving and the catering service started cleaning up. The band had left an hour earlier. When the last of the people were gone, it was nine o'clock. Rex and I sat down with Angelina and Cole.

"You girls out did yourselves. And you, Cole, what a surprise you had. We are so happy for the two of you."

"Thanks, Rex. We have a lot to decide like the wedding date and where. You know how big Angelina's family is."

"I know my father will insist on having the wedding at our ranch." Angelina added.

"Well, we need to be going.        Rex, I may want to talk to you about adding onto the cabin.

"You kids go home and we'll talk later," Rex replied giving Cole one of those guy hugs. I gave Angelina a hug and kiss on the cheek.

"I am beat, let's go to bed."

"I am right behind you," I replied.

We laid in bed, snuggling and talked for a while. "I think Cole wants to expand the cabin so he and Angelina can live there. If that's the case, I'll give them the cabin and some land for a wedding present."

"Isn't the cabin a bit small?"

"Sweetheart, they are young and in love."

With that we fell asleep.

# Chapter Eighteen

One rainy fall afternoon, I was strumming my guitar. Rex had taken a rare afternoon off and we were sitting in front of the fireplace. Why are you so glum?" he asked.

"I miss my piano," was all I said.

"One day we should go back to town and pick it up. Say, don't you have a birthday coming up?"

"Yes, but it always gets lost in the bustle of the holidays."

"It's December 20th, right?"

"Yep," and I went back to my guitar.

With Christmas a month away, I was busy decorating, shopping, planning meals and trying to figure out what to get Rex for Christmas. Out of desperation, I went to Cole. "I don't know what to get Rex for Christmas. Do you have any suggestions?"

"Take him on a trip somewhere. He never leaves this ranch."

"How about a cruise?"

"Negative. Rex likes his feet on the ground. I do have an idea though. Rex has never been to the Grand Canyon and he has lived here all of his life."

'I've never seen the Grand Canyon either so it would be a first for both of us. Thanks, Cole."

I researched places to stay at the Grand Canyon and found there were no rooms available over the holidays. I opted to leave the dates open-ended and we could decide when we wanted to go. More than anything, I was excited to have a gift for Rex.

Rex took me out for an elegant dinner on my birthday and gave me a dozen white roses. I was a little disappointed I didn't get a gift. On the other hand, my birthday had always conflicted with Christmas.

"What are we going to do for Christmas?" Rex asked.

"I thought we could have a nice brunch, just the two of us, and have Cole and Angelina over for dinner."

"That sounds great."

Christmas morning, it was cold and crisp outside. I wanted to stay cuddled up in bed. However, Rex would have no part of it. "Come on sleepy head, I am hungry and am going to start the coffee. Are you coming?"

I groaned, rolled over in bed and found my robe. "I am going to brush my teeth and will join you in the kitchen."

I brushed my teeth, combed my hair and washed my face. When I got to the kitchen, Rex was nowhere to be seen. I got a cup of coffee and went to the great room. Rex had turned on the lights of our eight-foot Christmas tree.

"Merry Christmas," he said with a big grin. He pointed to the tree and I saw a new baby grand piano with a huge red ribbon.

"Oh My Gosh, what is this?"

"It is your Christmas present. I believe you mentioned you missed your piano."

"I've always wanted a baby grand," I said putting my arms around his neck and giving him a hug and kiss.

"Well, now you have one. Aren't you going to try it out?"

"Of course." I lifted the lid and opened the keyboard. First, I played a few chords and then began play to Claire de Lune." It was perfectly tuned.

"How did you get it in here without me knowing about it?"

"Remember when we got back from dinner last night? You wanted to sit in the great room and I told you I was too tired and wanted to go to bed. Well, while we were at dinner, I had the piano delivered. I couldn't let you see it before this morning."

"That's rather clever and I love you so much. Oh, and I have something for you." I found my envelope and gave it to him.

"Don't tell me its money."

"No silly, you have enough money."

Rex opened the envelope and pulled out a brochure for the Grand Canyon. "Cole told me that you have never been to the Grand Canyon and neither have I, so I am taking you on a trip."

"Sweetheart, I can think of no better gift other than your little body snuggled up with me."

"Are you inviting me to snuggle?"

"That would be the game plan."

# Chapter Nineteen

Angelina and Cole set their wedding date for the following October. They would be married in a meadow on her father's ranch. She had four sisters and three brothers, all of whom would be in the wedding party. Cole was an only child and his parents had been divorced many years ago. His dad was flying in from Hawaii and his mother had remarried and declined the invitation. Cole had been living with Rex since he was five years old and he was more of a dad to him than his own father.

Rex and Cole were out on the range when Cole asked Rex to be his best man. "What about your father?" Rex asked.

"My dad has never been there for me, but you have."

When Rex told me about their conversation, he was beaming and I knew he was pleased and honored to be Cole's best man.

Rex gave Angelina and Cole the cabin plus ten acres of land as a wedding present. They had started remodeling the 1800's building and hoped it would be finished by the time they were married.

# Chapter Twenty

I couldn't get Rex to commit to a date for our trip to the Grand Canyon. "You know that reservations aren't easy to get, so it would be good to set a date."

Rex's hesitation was that calving happens in the spring and he needed to be there. "Can't Cole handle the calving along with the ranch hands? After all, if he is to take over the ranch one day, he needs to be given more responsibility."

"Darl'n you are absolutely right. That's what I love about you. You get me out of my ruts."

I called the El Tovar Hotel, built in 1905 and located on the south rim of the Grand Canyon. I was told that they were sold out for the next year. I asked to speak to the manager who told me the same thing until I asked to be added to their cancellation list and gave him Rex's full name. "Just a moment." The manager came back on line a few moments later. "I believe we can accommodate you the first week of May if that would work for you." I gave him my credit card to hold the room and thanked him profusely.

When I told Rex about my experience with the hotel manager, he smiled and said, "I'm pretty well known in this part of the country. When are we going?"

"The first week of May."

"Perfect. Thanks, Darl'n"

# Chapter Twenty-One

One beautiful day in March, I had the urge to go target shooting. I hadn't done any practice shooting since I met Rex and wanted to keep my skills proficient. When I asked Rex if I could shoot on the ranch and where I could shoot, he offered to go with me.

We rode off the following morning. I had become confident riding Lady and Rex was beside me on Honey. The guns and ammunition were in Rex's saddle bags and I had our lunch in my saddle bags. We rode for about an hour and then came upon a ridge that was perfect as a berm to stop our shots.

We dismounted and Rex handed me my shooting gear. "That is a pretty fancy rig you have there. Did someone make it for you?"

"Yep, when I got to Arizona and took up shooting, I wanted a cowboy revolver and the gun shop where I bought the gun had a leather tooler. He made the gun belt and holster for me. If you read the Cowboy Shooter magazine, I was on the front cover of the July issue a couple of years ago," I said proudly.

"Well, if that doesn't beat all! I am in the midst of a celebrity. Come on cowgirl, let me see you shoot."

I strapped on my gun belt and secured the holster to my leg. I loaded my Cimarron .38 special with six rounds of ammunition. Rex secured targets to a tree and I stepped off twenty-five feet. When Rex was safely behind me, I drew my pistol and shot off all six rounds grouping them dead center.

Rex let out a loud yeehaw. "Darl'n remind me never to mess with you,"

We shot for an hour or so. We weren't competing, but I was really a better shot than Rex and he let me have that.

"As the looser, I am going to buy you lunch."

"But we brought our lunch."

"Precisely."

"Okay, fancy pants. You pick a place for lunch and I'll race you there."

Rex took off on Honey at a gallop. I knew he would get to the grove of trees before I did.

"Okay, who is the best rider?" Rex asked grinning.

"Well, now it wouldn't be me."

# Chapter Twenty-Two

We hadn't talked much about our trip to the Grand Canyon but I was getting excited about the excursion. I confirmed our reservations and started making a mental list of the clothes I wanted to take.

"Rex, you know we leave on our trip in two weeks. Can you get the truck serviced before then?" Rex nodded and said he would take care of it.

The morning we were to leave for the Grand Canyon, I had our suitcases by the front door. Rex casually picked them up and carried them to the truck. Rex started the truck and we were off on our first vacation together. I had our itinerary with me and was reviewing our plans when Rex pulled into a small airport.

"Rex, what are we doing here?"

"Well, it's an airport and has airplanes. I thought it would be fun to fly to the Grand Canyon."

"You have got to be kidding. Who is going to fly the plane?"

"Well, if you trust me, I am."

"Do you have a license?"

"Of course. Are you game?"

"I have never flown in a plane this small."

"I figured the best way to see the Grand Canyon is with my best girl from the air. Come on, we need to go inside and record our flight plan."

"Do you own this airplane?"

"Yep."

This man never ceases to amaze and surprise me.

Sitting in the cockpit, Rex handed me a headset. "This is so we can talk to each other."

We were ready to taxi down the runway. Rex was totally concentrating on his flying controls. We picked up speed and then we were airborne. It was breathtaking.

"I'm going to fly over the ranch."

Rex made a 180 degree turn and in seconds we were over the ranch. I could see the ranch house, the cabin tucked in the trees and the cattle scattered over the land. It was larger than I had imagined.

"How many acres do you own?"

"Just under 20,000 square acres."

I couldn't compute in my brain how much land this was, but I knew it was a lot.

After the air tour of the ranch, Rex turned the plane in a northwest direction. We flew over forests, deserts and small towns along the way. "That's the old Route 66," he pointed out.

A few minutes later, I heard Rex talking to me. "You aren't supposed to fly into the Grand Canyon, but I got a special pass from the aeronautical folks."

The further north we got, the more spectacular the scenery. Once we were over the canyon, the geology became more prominent and beautiful. From my research, I learned that the Grand Canyon is 277 miles long, nearly 18 miles in width in some places and was carved by the Colorado River over billions of years.

After our bird's eye view of the canyon, Rex headed south in a flight pattern to the Grand Canyon Airport. Rex was now in contact with the traffic control tower for landing instructions. The airport was small with one runway and Rex landed the plane smoothly as we taxied to the designated parking area.

"So, how was it?"

"Sweetheart, that was fabulous and much more exciting

than driving."

We checked in with the flight control personnel and then rented a car, a cute red Mustang convertible. We immediately put the top down so we could enjoy the seven-mile drive to the entrance of the park.

Signs pointed us in the direction of the El Tovar Hotel. Registration was quick and the personnel more than friendly. Our bags were delivered just as we arrived at our room. When the bellhop opened the curtains, I gasped. We were on the rim side of the hotel and had our own personal view of the canyon.

"Did you do this?" I referred to the view.

As usual, Rex only smiled and then he picked me up and kissed me.

That night while Rex slept, I couldn't help but wonder when this fairytale would end.

We spent two nights at the Grand Canyon and decided to drive to Bryce Canyon and Zion National Park in Utah. The scenery was no less spectacular, but after another four days of looking at red rock we were ready to go home to the ranch.

When we got back home, Cole met us in the driveway. "Welcome home," he greeted us.

"How did things go while we were gone?"

"Not a hitch."

We all walked into the house and Cole whispered in my ear. "You were gone a week. I don't think Rex has ever been gone from the ranch that long."

I simply smiled at him and headed to the bedroom. I knew the men would talk business and I was in need of a hot shower.

# Chapter Twenty-Three

Rex wanted to go for a horseback ride one hot July day. I wasn't thrilled about riding in the hot sun, but agreed if we weren't out too long. Rex saddled Honey and Lady and we rode toward the cabin. The cabin was under construction, but no one was working that day.

"This is the first place we rode almost a year ago," I commented.

"I remember. Let's tie up the horses and sit under the trees and cool off."

We tied up the horses and put out a blanket under the trees. Rex was anxious about something. He was usually so sure of himself.

"Is something wrong?" I asked.

"No. It's just me."

"Do you want to talk about it?"

"I think we need to."

Oops, is this my fairytale coming to an end?

"Darl'n, we have been together now for a year."

Here it comes.

"And, I have never been happier."

What is he trying to say? "Are you trying to tell me something?"

Rex sat down beside me, took my hands and said, "What I am trying to tell you is that I love you with all my heart. Would you marry me?"

"Is that what you have been so nervous about? Of course, I will marry you and want more than anything to be your wife."

"So, is that a 'yes'?"

"Now just what do you think? Yes, yes and yes." I said as I pulled him down on the blanket and kissed him.

As we laid there, Rex whispered in my ear, "You have made me a very happy man." Suddenly Rex was sitting up. "I nearly forgot, I have this for you."

He dug in his jean pocket and came out with a small tissue wrapped object. I unwrapped it and found a perfect diamond engagement ring. "The diamond is huge, how big is it?"

"Three carats. Is that big enough?"

"I wouldn't care how big it is, it is beautiful and I love you."

We talked about when we would get married and decided not to take away from Angelina and Cole's wedding in October. "How about a Christmas wedding?" I suggested.

"Do you want a traditional wedding?" He asked.

"If the truth be known, we are such private people, I would rather not. What do you want to do?"

It didn't take Rex long to answer. "I had a big wedding before and it is a lot of work and the bride and groom are worn out before the ceremony. What would you think of going to the mountains and finding a chapel? There will be snow in December and we can spend a few days to ourselves."

"Do you know I couldn't think of a more sentimental wedding?"

"Then it is a deal. Would you mind researching cabins?"

"For you, my darling, it would be my pleasure."

The heat was getting intense, so we headed back on our horses. My new engagement ring glimmered in the sun reflecting the love in my heart for this wonderful man.

My fairytale life is not coming to an end.

We were married on Christmas Day in the mountains. We had no relatives or friends in attendance. Rex requested a simple wedding band and he added a diamond band to my engagement ring. We wrote our wedding vows and recited them together.

## We Fell In Love

*We searched for love,*
*And found love with each other.*
*In this sweet time of our lives,*
*We are coming together.*
*To declare our love and devotion.*

*I, Roxie, take you, Rex, as my lawful wedded husband,*
*To love and cherish for the rest of our lives.*
*I, Rex, take you, Roxie, as my lawful wedded wife,*
*To love and cherish for the rest of our lives.*

Rex and I returned to the ranch and announced we had been married. No one asked why we didn't have a big wedding, no words needed to be said.

Life was blissful and our relationship grew stronger each day. I found my creative side had opened up and I wrote more and more songs. I watched the kittens grow into wonderful, loving cats. Angela and Cole were married and had a beautiful ceremony. Cole learned more about the ranch and Rex was taking more time off.

One day we were sitting on the patio reminiscing about our past years. We had just celebrated our tenth wedding anniversary. I gently held Rex's hand and smiled. Fairy tales do come true.

# Epilogue

Rex and Roxie lived at the ranch for another ten years together. One night while he slept next to his beloved wife, Rex had a massive heart attack and died in his sleep. He was ninety-six years old. Roxie moved into the cabin and Angelina and Cole moved into the ranch house with their two children, ages five and seven.

Roxie continued with her music and often rode Lady, who had also gotten old around the ranch pastures where she and Rex had spent wonderful excursions together. At the age of ninety, Roxie wrote her last song to Rex the day before she died.

*YOU ARE HERE*

*You are here I know,*
*Like the softness of fallen snow.*
*Like angel wings upon the wind,*
*My fairy tale story has no end.*

*I feel you with me in the night,*
*When loneliness waits for light.*
*Your shadows are wisps of cotton,*
*Your whispers are unforgotten.*

*Your smile is forever with me,*
*Your love has set me free.*
*You are here I know,*
*Waiting for my time to go.*

The End

# When Love
# Comes to Us

# Introduction

"We always take the same vacation every year. It's either to Hawaii or Mexico. Why don't we ditch the beaches and do a hike in the mountains."

"Because we don't know anything about hiking."

"Then we should do some research, hike the hills around here and get some experience."

We had the same conversation every year. I was a beach lover and Sam went with me because, well because he just went with me. However, this year he was insistent upon an inland excursion. It was January and time to plan our annual vacation.

# Chapter One

We met five years ago in San Francisco. Sam was playing at Fisherman's Wharf for a charity event. I was spending the weekend with my life-time girlfriend, Gretchen, in Sausalito who suggested we attend the concert. I wasn't much on watching a bunch of wanna-be musicians playing guitars and drums, but I agreed to go.

Gretchen and I took the ferry from Sausalito to Fisherman's Wharf. Even though it was July, the weather was cool and damp from the bay water breeze. Upon arrival at the dock, we deported doing our best to ignore vendors selling trinkets and food.

The concert was scheduled for six o'clock and it was now just five o'clock. Gretchen suggested we grab a bite to eat before going to the concert. With crab and shrimp cocktails in Styrofoam cups and wine in plastic cups (this culinary delight really excited me) we walked the block to where the band was scheduled to play.

We couldn't miss the band because they were warming up producing sounds that hurt my ears. There was a good looking fellow on guitar, someone on keyboard and a third guy on saxophone. Great, I thought, this is just what I wanted to do while visiting San Francisco. Gretchen knew that I was unhappy, but she wasn't willing to pick up and leave.

We found seats on a picnic bench and Gretchen and I chatted about my recent law cases and she filled me in on her students at the university where she taught journalism. As the clock struck six o'clock, the band began to play and I heard the most melodious sounds. They played Janis Joplin, Frank Sinatra and even a little bit of Elvis. I was mesmerized and watched the guitarist play with all of his heart. He didn't just play, he lived what he played.

"Who is that guitar player?" I asked.

"Oh, that's Sam. Didn't I tell you I know him? He's one of my journalism students."

"That means he's young."

"Nope. He decided after not making a living at playing the guitar and singing, he would take up his second passion and that would be journalism."

"How old is he?"

"I don't know for sure, but probably about your age. Do you want to meet him on break?"

I was definitely interested in meeting this attractive, talented fellow. "I suppose that would be okay," I said trying to hide my excitement.

It was another forty-five minutes before the band announced they were taking a break. Gretchen motioned for me to follow her as we walked towards the band.

"Gretchen, I am so happy you made our concert." Sam said. "Is this the friend you told me about?"

"Sam, this is Julie. She is visiting me from Sacramento."

Sam gave me a California surfer smile and extended his hand. As I took his hand in a hand shake, it was his ocean blue eyes that captured me. Finally, thinking I had held his hand long enough, I broke the grasp and eye contact.

"So, what are you girls doing while Julie is visiting?"

"Just doing a lot of girl catch-up. Say, if you aren't doing anything tomorrow, how about coming over to my place for a cookout? I am having a bunch of folks over for a seafood feast."

"Sounds great. What time?"

"Any time after four o'clock and bring your guitar and the other band members."

"I'll be there. See you tomorrow. I need to get something to drink and hit the head before our next set."

"What was all that about?" I inquired, "Asking him to come to the cookout. You know that I will still be here?"

"Of course, silly. That's why I asked him. I think you two could hit it off."

I didn't think much about the next evening, or Sam. After all, I lived in Sacramento and was an aspiring lawyer. What would I want with a guitar player studying to be a journalist?

Gretchen had invited ten or so couples for the cookout. She had a number of friends who were scuba divers and dove for the abalone we were going to eat that evening. "Can you dive for abalone all year long?" I asked Jerry, one of the scuba divers.

"Nope, ab can only be hunted from April to November and not in July."

"How many can you take?"

"There is a limit of three abs a day per diver and not more than twenty-four in a year. That's why we have so many divers today. We have a lot of people to feed."

While the divers were harvesting the abalone, others were fishing for whatever fish can be caught from the pier. Not only did the divers and fishermen provide the food, but they took over the cooking for the evening. Gretchen and I only had to pick up sour dough bread, appetizers and salads from the deli that afternoon.

The party was announced as informal and Gretchen's friends probably wouldn't know how to dress if it was anything but informal. The guys had longish hair, wore shorts and some were without shirts or shoes of any kind. The women also sported long hair, floor length skirts and jewelry from the sixties. I quickly went into the bedroom and changed out of my conservative shorts and top to jean shorts and a t-shirt. "I wondered if you would change your clothes," Gretchen grinned at me.

As the couples arrived, bottles of wine and beer were being opened. I was introduced to everyone, but couldn't have called them by name two minutes later. Ten or fifteen minutes into the party, I felt an arm around my shoulders. "Julie, it's good to see you." It was Sam and he looked good enough to eat. His shoulder length blonde hair was shiny and smelled of shampoo. He had on a Hawaiian shirt and khaki shorts that showed off his tan body. He didn't get that tan in the Bay area. I remembered his marvelous blue eyes and captivating smile from the night before. What I didn't remember was that he was about 6'2" tall. This was good because at 5'10" I was often taller than a lot of men.

"It's good to see you too. Did you bring your guitar?" Julie asked.

"Does a cowboy ride a horse?"

"I guess that means you brought your guitar. Where is the rest of your band?"

"They couldn't come, so I am the sole entertainment. I'm going to set up by the fire ring," Sam said as he started to walk away. Looking back at me, he asked, "Are you coming?"

A little surprised at his boldness, I managed to reply, "Uh, of course. Let me get my wine and I will be right there."

Sam was tuning his guitar when I met up with him. I sat down on a stack of blankets and settled in. Sam didn't say anything and neither did I. It seemed like he tuned his guitar forever. Why does it take so long to tune up a couple of strings? When he was ready to play, I once again heard that melodious sound. So, it was Sam and the guitar I heard last night in perfect harmony. He sang songs by The Kingston Trio followed by Simon and Garfunkel. I found I was soon singing. Sam looked over at me and I blushed. I had never sung in public before.

I was so absorbed in Sam's singing that I forgot there were other people around. It really didn't matter because they weren't aware of me either and Gretchen, being the good hostess she was, socialized with everyone.

Suddenly the music stopped and I found I had laid back on the blankets. My wine glass was empty and my eyes were shut. "Are you asleep?" Sam asked touching my arm.

"Uh, no. Your music is so relaxing and I must have almost fallen asleep." I said sitting up and laughing.

"I'm going take a break. Care to go with me?"

"I 'd love to as soon as I refill my wine glass. Can I get you another beer?"

"Sure. I'll go to the kitchen with you."

We got our drinks and went out on the deck. It was a beautiful summer night. The stars were bright and the weather cooperated with a light breeze. Sam suggested we walk along the boardwalk to a small park down the street. I was only too happy to get away from the noise and crowd. As we walked, Sam asked if I was going home in the morning.

"Nope, I'm on a long-overdue weeks' vacation from work. I've been visiting Gretchen in the summertime since she moved to Sausalito five years ago."

The park overlooked the San Francisco Bay and the view of the Golden Gate Bridge was spectacular. "Since you are a returning visitor, I won't spend time pointing out the tourist sites across the bay."

"No," I laughed. I'd rather talk with you. Gretchen tells me you are one of her journalism students. What kind of journalism do you write?"

"I would write most anything right now if someone would pay me." Sam was smiling. "The fact is that until I get a degree in journalism, I remain unemployed except for my music. There are so many wanna-be journalists in the Bay area that jobs are few and far between."

"Then why not transfer schools?"

"I suppose laziness is an excuse, but not a very good one. I like living in the city. It's exciting and I can get gigs pretty easily."

"What's a gig?"

"It's a live performance and generally involves one or more

entertainers. I like to get paid, but I also do performances for no pay, like the one last night for charity.

"So, what kind of journalist do you want to be?"

"I'd like to start off with a newspaper and get experience in several venues writing columns and covering stories. If the truth be known, human rights are a passion of mine, but I don't think I can get enough of that kind of work with one newspaper. At some point, I would like to go freelance. Then there is the issue of salary, which isn't great starting out. I figure I can supplement my income with my music."

It was getting dark and the breeze off the bay was chilly. "I'd love to know more about your ambitions, but right now I'm getting cold"

"Must be your Sacramento blood." Sam said as we got off the park bench and headed back to the house.

"How did you know I was from Sacramento?"

"Well, I know that and that you are a lawyer. You are twenty-eight years old and you and Gretchen have been friends forever. Oh, and you are single. Does that cover the important parts?"

"You and Gretchen must have had a conversation?"

"Yep."

"Well, that puts me at a disadvantage. How do I get to learn more about you?"

"I am twenty-nine years old and grew up in San Diego. I moved to San Francisco just after I graduated from high school to go to San Francisco State University and study music. I quickly learned there are more musicians than gigs or jobs in the Bay area, so I decided to get a second degree in journalism. I'm in my fourth year and hope to graduate early in the fall."

"What about your family?"

"I'm the fifth of six children. My dad is a neurosurgeon and my mother is a pediatric doctor. They both still work and swear they will never retire. "

We talked until everyone started to leave. Several people asked

Sam why he didn't play anymore. Sam simply waved his hand in the air and gave them one of his charming smiles.

"Would you like to take a drive through Napa Valley tomorrow and visit a couple of wineries? It's usually busy with people and cars, but being it's a Monday we might luck out."

"I'd love to go. Gretchen is teaching in summer school, so I'm free."

We made plans for Sam to pick me up at eight the following morning. Why did I meet this fellow on vacation when he lived in San Francisco and I lived in Sacramento? This wasn't going to work, or so I thought as I fell asleep.

# Chapter Two

The Bay area is often cool and overcast in the early hours in the month of June. True to form, it was chilly when Sam picked me up. He drove a new bright red Jeep. When I commented on his Jeep, he told me he didn't get much work, but he wasn't poor.

The trip from Sausalito to Napa Valley takes two hours and we chatted about the places he and his band played. He turned the conversation to me and asked about my law practice.

"I practice family law with six other lawyers in a family law firm in downtown Sacramento."

"What kind of cases do you take?"

"Being a family lawyer means we take any case related to family affairs such as divorce, alimony, child support and prenuptial cases."

"Sounds pretty diverse."

"That's why I like it. I also like that I can help people when marriages don't work out. It's not always the guy who ends up paying alimony. Women can get the shaft too."

We arrived in Napa and were faced with streets full of cars and sidewalks busy with tourist. "I didn't realize how this area had grown. Do you know how many wineries there are now?"

"Not exactly, but we can ask at one of the wineries if you're interested."

Sam suddenly turned into a fast-food place. "Hungry?"

"Not this hungry."

"I was only kidding. It's getting close to lunch time and I wondered if you had ever taken the train ride through the wine country?"

"No, but I've heard it's awesome."

"You usually need reservations well in advance. Let's give it a try." Sam got back on the road and started following signs to the Napa Train Ride. I wasn't sure we could get tickets, but then I am known to be a pessimistic person.

We drove into the train depot and found the parking lot was packed. After driving around for a few minutes, we spotted someone pulling out and we snagged the space. "This has got to be an omen," Sam said smiling as he parked the car. He was out of the Jeep in seconds. "Come on Julie, we don't have much time to catch the eleven o'clock train."

Sam took ahold of my hand and we ran to the depot. There was no one in line and I just knew we wouldn't get tickets. "Tickets for two on the eleven o'clock train," Sam told the ticket agent. The agent looked at us and said, "Would you believe two people just cancelled their tickets. They are for first class, but I can give you a discount because the other couple didn't get a refund."

Sam got out his credit card and paid for the tickets. "How did you do that?" I asked.

"Babes, when you think positive thoughts, good things happen. When we walked up to the ticket agent, I said a mantra in my head. 'We will get tickets, we will get tickets' and it worked."

"I hope we get lunch. I'm starving."

Boarding the train, Sam glanced at the brochure the ticket agent had given him. "It says here that we get a meal in the Petite Gourmet Car on the way through Napa Valley. On the way back, we get coffee and dessert in the lounge car."

Twenty minutes into our trip, we were escorted to another car where we were to have lunch. The dining room was luxurious with white table cloths adorned with flowers. Every table sat next to a window for an up close and personal view of the vineyards. "This is fabulous," I said as Sam pulled out my chair.

We ordered a glass of wine and looked over the menu. "Would you believe this, Sam? We have a choice of filet mignon, grilled salmon, pork tenderloin, or chicken breast?"

We both ordered the baby lettuce salad with walnuts and gorgonzola cheese as an appetizer and the filet mignon served on a truffle potato cake as our entree. The meal was as excellent as any 5-star restaurant and we were on a train!

"Sam, this was an absolutely wonderful idea. The scenery is beautiful and we couldn't have seen this much from the Jeep. Not to mention that the meal is beyond anything my hunger could imagine." I reached over and touched the top of his hand, "Thank you."

My hand was being turned over and I felt the same warm grasp I felt the first time we shook hands. "You are more than welcome."

"Excuse me," the waiter interrupted, "Would you care for coffee?"

We were drinking our coffee when the conductor announced that the train was being turned around in St. Helena and we were to move to the lounge car on the way back to the train station. We were seated at a small round table for two covered with a white table cloth and sat in captain chairs covered in red velvet. The waiter asked if we would like an after-dinner drink with our dessert.

"What would you like, Julie?"

"Cognac sounds heavenly."

"Make that two," Sam told the waiter.

The train ride back seemed so much shorter than the trip up. When I mentioned this to Sam, he agreed saying trips are always like that. It was three in the afternoon when we got back to Napa.

"Let's walk around the town and work off some of this food and alcohol. Otherwise, I won't be able to drive home." I was glad for the opportunity to stretch my legs. We bought a bottle of local wine and cheese at one of the wine stores. Most of the stores were tourist traps and I had no reason to buy any trinkets.

# Chapter Three

An hour later, we were back on the road to Sausalito. We were awake, but had no energy to do anything but enjoy the two-hour trip home. I didn't want the day to end and asked Sam in for a glass of wine or a cup of coffee. I wondered if he had his guitar with him.

"I had hoped you would ask me in. I don't want to call it a day this soon. I brought my guitar, should I bring it in the house?"

"Absolutely! It's still early, how about we sit on the deck. And yes, I would love to hear you play and sing. Can I get you a glass of wine, or I can make a pot of coffee?"

"Why don't you open that bottle of wine we got today? It is a Cabernet Sauvignon from a new wine region and I'd like to try it. I'll meet you on the deck."

I carried out the wine and two glasses. "Are you hungry?"

"Not really, maybe we can nibble on that cheese later on. What would you like to hear?"

"Hmmm," I was running through the folk music file in my mind. "How about something by Woodie Guthrie?"

Sam began strumming 'This Land is Your Land'. I knew the words and started singing along with Sam.

As he had done at last night's party, he looked at me and smiled. Sam played for a while singing songs by such singers as Gordon Lightfoot, John Denver, and Joan Baez. When he stopped playing, I asked him why he played folk music.

"Folk music tells a story about people. These stories are usually not written down, but are told by word of mouth. If you listen, really listen, you will hear those stories. I've always been about causes and that's what folk music is all about. Do you really want to hear this because I can talk music all night?"

"Absolutely," as I filled up our wine glasses.

"Listen to the words," Sam said as he began to play and sing 'Blow'n in the Wind'.

"I've never really listened to the words and what they mean. It sounds like a protest song."

"Dylan tells us that it is not a protest song. However, your interpretation is how you feel about the meaning of the words."

"I hear it as a cry for freedom from the blacks or any other culture and that the answer to their freedom is unknown at the time, or blown' in the wind."

"Julie, that's exactly correct. Dylan wrote the song after an old African spiritual asking why their people were enslaved. Would you like to hear another one?"

"Sure. Hmm, how about 'Puff the Magic Dragon'?"

"That would be a song Peter, Paul and Mary made famous."

I listened intently at the words trying to find meaning in them. When in actuality, the song seemed quite simplistic and clear. Sam finished playing and looked at me. "Well?"

"I remember loving this song and always thought it was a mystical child's song. To me, it's the story of a child who has an imaginary friend, the dragon. Jackie and the dragon are friends in the land of Honalee until Jackie grows up and leaves. The dragon, being left alone, goes back into his cave."

"Yes, it tells the story of most of us as we transgress from childhood to adulthood. The dragon protected Jackie Paper and they lived in a fictional land called Honalee. The kings and princes who came to see Jackie and the dragon were awed by their presence which gave both Jackie and the dragon power and courage. Puff became vulnerable when Jackie left him. He no longer had power to protect and went back to his cave to live."

"What a marvelous interpretation. Do you do this with the rest of your songs?"

"Mostly. What I mostly need to do is pack up and go home. I have a run with a group of guys that get together every Monday at six in the morning. If I don't get home, I won't have the energy to keep up with them." Sam began to gather his guitar and belongings. He finished his wine, stood up and offered me his hand. As I got up, he took me in his arms and kissed me on the cheek. "Julie, this was one of the most memorable days I've ever had. I have classes until noon tomorrow, but I would like to see you in the afternoon."

"That works perfect for me." My heart was beating fast and my knees were weak. "I had planned to go shopping at Union Square in the morning. Is there somewhere I can meet you after you get out of your classes?"

"Yeah, there's a Starbuck's on the corner of Powell and O'Farrell just a block from Union Square. Would that work for you?"

"Yes, it would," I said smiling. Sam looked at me and I thought he was going to kiss me. Instead, he released his hold and told me he would see me tomorrow afternoon.

Gretchen had come home from teaching and was quietly drinking a glass of wine in the kitchen. "I didn't know you were here," I exclaimed in surprise.

"Well, I wasn't going to interrupt you two love birds."

"Come on, Gretchen. We only spent the day together."

"OK what's up with the smile from ear to ear?"

I proceeded to fill her in on the day, all the while Gretchen was smiling. "I knew you two would hit it off. Are you going to see each other again? After all, you have another five days here."

"I'm meeting Sam after his classes tomorrow. Isn't Sam in your class? Do you want to join us?"

"Yes, Sam is in my class and no, I am not going to join you. I set you up to meet Sam and I'm not going to interfere with the two of you in romantic San Francisco.

Gretchen and I sat up until midnight talking and polished off a bottle of wine. I was exhausted when I finally went to bed and couldn't get Sam and the wonderful day we had out of my mind. I had the same thoughts I had the night before. Why did I meet Sam on vacation when he lived in San Francisco and I lived in Sacramento?

# Chapter Four

It was a beautiful summer day in the Bay area when I woke up on Monday. Gretchen and I had coffee on the deck admiring the Golden Gate Bridge and watching the seagulls wing their way on pockets of air currents hunting for their breakfast. "How did you find this place?"

"Remember the dive I rented when I moved to Sausalito? My landlord sold that place and I had to move. A friend of mine has this fabulous realtor who lists homes exclusively in Sausalito. His name is Jeff and when I told him my price range, he was skeptical he could find a place I could afford. I only had two months to relocate and I didn't want to rent again. Jeff called me one day and told me he just got this listing and would I be interested. We met when I got off work and I fell in love with the house and view. Of course, I ended up paying nearly twice what I had planned. However, I just couldn't pass this up regardless of the fact I am now dirt poor. Oops, look at the time. I need to get dressed for work and out of here. Do you want to take the ferry with me?"

"No, I have a little extra time. The stores don't open until ten o'clock. I'll see you this evening."

"If you decide to stay in the city this evening, just give me a call."

I drank another cup of coffee and tried to sort out the feelings I was developing for Sam. I knew little about him, but liked what I did know. He was nice looking, smart, kind, considerate, funny and most of all he was sensitive. Was that the musician in him? Without his direction, I would have never thought to listen to the words of a song let alone interpret the meaning of those words. And he believed in human rights. That wasn't any different than the rights I fought for with my clients. Well, it is getting late and I should get dressed and head out to Union Square and all of those shops that are calling for my credit cards.

I didn't know what Sam had in mind for the afternoon but knew whatever I wore would be appropriate in a tourist town. I had a new sundress and cover up I bought in Sacramento before I left. My mother always told me that a new outfit made a girl feel pretty and she was right. My long dark hair and blue eyes popped when I put on the fuchsia sundress. I carefully selected my accessories and make up. The full-length mirror in the guest bedroom confirmed indeed I did look pretty.

The ferry ride to Fisherman's Wharf was enjoyable as I stood on the deck with the salty breeze in my face. I took a taxi to Union Square and arrived just as the stores were opening. I have three hours to shop which is about the time my credit cards would hold out. My first stop was Nordstrom and I purchased a Hobo handbag. Thinking I would have to carry this large parcel with me the rest of the morning, the sales associate told me I could have any purchased item mailed to my home. Bingo! This was my ticket to more purchases. I found this mail-to-your-house policy was effective in most of the stores, especially the larger stores. Looking at my cell phone for the time, I found I had shopped for two and a half hours. It was time to head for Starbuck's. That is after I found a ladies' room to freshen up.

I arrived at Starbuck's two minutes to one and found Sam sitting outside drinking coffee. He saw me instantly. Had he been looking for me? "Julie," I heard him say, I'm over here." I smiled and found myself excited to see this lovely specimen of a man anxious to greet me.

"Hi there. Have you been here long?"

"No, just long enough to get a cappuccino. Would you like one?"

"No, not this late in the day. I'm hungry, though. Have you had lunch?"

"Not yet. Where are all of your bags? Didn't you go shopping?"

"Yes, and I did buy some things. The remarkable thing is the stores will mail them to you. Thus, I have my hands free this afternoon."

"I know you have been here before, but I would like to go down to Fisherman's Wharf. There are a couple of casual restaurants and I love going to the water."

"Lead the way," I said smiling and extending my hand. Sam took my hand and we walked to a trolley depot at Union Square that would take us to the Wharf. Sam holding my hand was nice and I found I liked the physical contact. The cable car ride wasn't long, but was very nostalgic. "What do you know about the history of the cable cars?" I asked.

"Hmm, let's see. The cable car system was built in the late 1800's because so many horses fell and died on the steep San Francisco hills."

"Oh dear, that's terrible for the horses."

"It was and the cable cars were short lived because the electric cars replaced them in the early 1900's."

The cable car was slowing to a stop. "Okay, let's see where we can find a place to fill up that empty stomach of yours. What kind of food would you like?"

"Seafood, of course." Sam resumed our hand holding as we walked down the wharf. We walked for thirty minutes and didn't see an acceptable eating establishment.

"I have an idea. Let's go to my place and I'll fix you lunch."

"You have got to be kidding. How far away do you live?"

"I share an apartment with another journalism student on the Presidio."

The Presidio was up there with the cost of the shiny red Jeep Sam owned. My curiosity was piqued and I agreed to the new lunch plans.

We took a five-minute taxi ride to Sam's place. It amazed me that everyone who lives in San Francisco thought nothing of taking a taxi. However, driving a car and parking is a monster nightmare. We pulled up in front of an immaculately maintained house with a front porch view of the ocean. I was in awe.

"This is home," Sam said as he led me up the walkway to the front door. "Make yourself at home and I'll start lunch. I walked around the house and found a large window in the living room looking out to the ocean. There were three bedrooms and two bathrooms. Two of the bedrooms were obviously occupied as evidenced by the messy bed clothes and dirty laundry on the floor.

I used the bathroom in the hallway and was amazed at how clean it was. I wandered out to the kitchen where Sam was furiously cutting up veggies. "Do you have a cleaning lady?"

"You betcha. Neither Dave, my roommate, nor I want to clean. Ruby comes in twice a week and makes us look good."

"Well, she does a great job. What are you making?"

"It is a specialty of mine. Stir fried shrimp with vegetables over rice."

"Sounds yummy. What can I do?"

"We keep cooked rice in the fridge. If you can get it out, it is on the right in the front, and reheat it, that would be great." When the vegetables were al dente, Sam set the table in the kitchen nook which just happened to overlook the water. He then added the shrimp to the vegetables and stir fried the contents of the skillet. "You can get a bottle of white wine from the bottom shelf of the refrigerator and open it. The corkscrew is in the drawer by the fridge and glasses are in the cabinet above."

Within thirty minutes, lunch was ready and on the table. I was impressed. "The meal is scrumptious and I love this wine. What is it?"

"It is a Pinot Grigio from Sonoma Valley."

"It is very good and so is the meal. This is ever so much better than fighting for a table and waiting an hour to get served."

"Thank you for the compliment. I love to cook and would rather eat at home than go out. Let's pour the rest of the wine and go outside."

The weather had been magnificent since I arrived and today was no different. We sat in lawn chairs and talked, not about anything serious, but about his school classes and what it was like growing up in a large family. "Julie, you haven't said anything about your family."

"There really isn't much to say. I'm an only child and my parents divorced when I was ten years old. I went to stay with my mother. My dad was getting remarried, which is the reason my parents divorced. When I was sixteen, my mother died of breast cancer and I had to go live with my dad and step mother. Terry, my step mother, was very nice. It's just that it was hard to adapt to a new living arrangement at sixteen. I was at home for another two years. By that time, I had decided to become a lawyer and specialize in family affairs. After all, I had lived it myself. I don't see my dad and Terry much. They live in Los Angeles and are busy with their lives. I left home after high school graduation and haven't been back since."

"WOW! I can't imagine living as an only child. What I remember most about growing up was the chaos every day and spats I had with my siblings."

"Do you see your family much?"

"Yes, we all get together at least once a year in San Diego. A couple of times, we have been to Hawaii. I try to get back one more time during the year." Sam looked at the clock. "Did you know its five o'clock? There are only two more ferries to Sausalito. We had better get going."

Waiting for the ferry, Sam put his arm around my waist and I rested my head on his shoulder. He was humming 'What is This Thing Called Love' and nuzzling my hair. This all felt so good and like the right thing to do.

"I don't have school tomorrow. Would you like to take a drive to Carmel-By-The-Sea and Monterey?"

"How can a girl refuse such an offer?"

The ferry was pulling up to the dock. "Great, I will pick you up at

Gretchen's at eight o'clock. Don't eat breakfast and bring a light wrap in case it's chilly." The ferry was blowing its horn to indicate it was time to board. I turned to Sam and put my arms around his neck. "Two wonderful days in two days. I will see you tomorrow." I gave him a lingering kiss which he returned.

Gretchen was waiting up for me when I returned. "So how did it go today?"

"I shopped and then met Sam. He took me back to his place and fixed me lunch. I have never had a guy cook for me before. Did you know he lived on the Presidio?"

"No, I didn't. Isn't that a bit pricey?"

"He lives with a roommate and I didn't ask what it cost to live there. Tomorrow we're going to Carmel and Monterey. I'm assuming that you are teaching tomorrow?"

"Yes, I am and even if I wasn't it is perfectly okay if you spend the day with Sam. Let's go out on the deck and watch the sun go down. Should I assume you had a late lunch and don't want dinner."

"You assumed correctly."

We sat outside and watched the sun as it dipped into the ocean's horizon. "You like Sam, don't you?"

"Yes, I do. After I broke up with Tony last year, I swore off men. I needed to get my life back. Unfortunately, I have been spending too much time on my practice and not enough time on my personal life. It has been so nice to be with a guy that treats me like a lady and makes me feel special."

"Well, girlfriend, you are special and I'm happy that you're having a good time. Never mind that I am working every day while you are out playing."

"You brat," I said throwing my wadded-up cocktail napkin at her. We laughed, as good friends do.

I went to bed that night exhausted, but exhilarated. I thought about Tony and how he manipulated me and took advantage of our relationship. When we broke up, I didn't know if I could trust a man again. Then I met Sam and he was so sweet and honest. With those thoughts, I fell into a deep sleep.

# Chapter Five

I woke up early the next morning. Gretchen was still asleep. I made a pot of coffee and sat out on the deck. I loved coming to Sausalito even though I wasn't too crazy about the tourists or the way people got around without a car.

"Hey," Gretchen greeted me as she sat down with a cup of coffee. "How did you sleep?"

"Like a baby, and you?"

"Just as good. Do you think you and Sam will be out all day?"

"I would think so. Why, did you have plans?"

"I thought I would stay in the city after I get off work and do some shopping. Bill called late last night and asked if I wanted to get together for dinner around eight o'clock."

"Who is Bill?"

"A fellow I met at a school function a couple of months ago. He also works for the university in the English department. He's a nice guy and I enjoy his company. We usually go out once a week, or so. It's seven o'clock, shouldn't you be getting ready?"

"Oh, my goodness, I need to hustle." I had an hour to shower and get dressed. For once I appreciated living out of suitcase because it limited my selection of outfits to wear. I showered, put on a pair of white Capri pants with a sleeveless top and matching cover-up shirt. Just as I was finishing my makeup, Sam arrived looking like he walked out of a California surfing magazine. His blonde hair was a bit

103

windblown and he wore his signature Hawaiian shirt and Khaki shorts.

"Good morning, Julie. Are you ready to go?"

"Good morning to you too and yes, I'm ready to go." I yelled goodbye to Gretchen and we headed out.

We drove across the Golden Gate Bridge and even though traffic was going into town, at eight-thirty the bulk of the traffic had subsided. We picked up the 1 Freeway that runs down the coast. "There's a great little place to have breakfast just out of the city in Rockaway Beach. They have the best omelets."

We drove in silence for a while. Sam broke the quiet when he asked me why I decided to practice law in Sacramento.

"I grew up in Los Angeles and wanted to get away from the crowds and traffic. So, I went to law school in Sacramento. I had also taken the California Bar exam and didn't want to go through the stress of taking another bar exam in another state. Then I got an offer from Larson, Thompson and Smith Law Firm in Sacramento. I like living in the state capital where laws are made. You might like it there being so close to the government officials and being able to speak up for human rights."

"I don't know. I would miss the ocean and City. Here we are," Sam pointed out the restaurant. It was a quaint looking place with a small parking lot that was nearly full. We lucked out and got a table on the bayside. "The omelets are huge and I would suggest we split one."

"Works for me and I can eat most anything. Your choice."

Sacramento didn't come up again and that was okay with me. Sam paid the bill and we got back on the road. I would like to pick up a tab, but don't want to be offensive. Perhaps I can pick up lunch.

Along the drive to Monterey, we pulled over to see the seals and pelicans playing in the surf and sun. "Seals are so funny looking and smell terrible," I said laughing.

"You'd smell too if you had a coat of blubber to keep you warm," Sam said putting his arm around me.

In Monterey, we parked the car and walked to Cannery Row named after John Steinbeck. "I remember a great restaurant built out over the water."

Sam thought for a moment. "That would be the Fish Hopper. It's after twelve o'clock and won't be too crowded. We could stop for a glass of wine."

"That would be great. Use your positive mantra to get us a window seat."

"Nope, it is your turn to use positive thinking to get us a table."

"Okay, I'm game. 'There is a window table for us, there is a window table for us', I chanted with my eyes closed and thought positively. After all, I couldn't fail on my first solo attempt at this skill. The waiter told us to follow him and he led us to a window seat over the water.

"Way to go, sweetheart," Sam gave me a squeeze and one of his California surfing smiles.

"It worked. I'll be damned." Did Sam just call me sweetheart?

The rest of the day was heavenly. We spent two hours in the Monterey Bay Aquarium. I kept returning to the outside pools with the otters. "Sam, they are so adorable and playful. I want to take one home." Sam just chuckled. It was four o'clock when we left the aquarium.

"Are you up for a trip to Carmel-By-The-Sea for dinner? We didn't get lunch and I am starved, how about you?"

"I could have eaten one of those fish in the aquarium."

"Yuck! I will take that as a yes for dinner." The coast line was as beautiful as I remembered it with its high cliffs and crashing surf. We parked the Jeep downtown and walked to find a restaurant. We both agreed on an oyster bar and dined on oysters on the half shell, calamari, crab cakes, shrimp and a bottle of Chardonnay wine. It was eight o'clock when we left the restaurant and headed back to Sausalito.

"Are you okay to drive? We could stop and get a cup of coffee."

"I'll be fine. How about you join me singing to keep us both awake?"

"Are you serious? You want me to sing?"

"I've heard you sing and you have a wonderful voice."

"Then I would love to join you."

Two hours later Sam dropped me off at Gretchen's. Neither one of us wanted to say good night. Sam gave me a hug and kissed me affectionately. "I've wanted to do that all day," he said.

"Me too."

"Would you like to come over for dinner after you get out of school tomorrow?"

"Who's cooking?"

"I am. Does that change your mind?"

"No, just checking. Is four o'clock a good time?"

I said good night to Sam and watched him walk to the Jeep. Gretchen wasn't home and I was thankful for some quiet time to myself. When I went to bed, I didn't wonder why I had met Sam when he lived in San Francisco and I lived in Sacramento. I knew why fate had brought us together and knew we needed to talk about it soon.

# Chapter Six

Dinner the following night was a success. I made my famous lasagna with a salad, sour dough bread and Cabernet Sauvignon wine. I invited Gretchen to join us and she gratefully accepted the invitation. After all, I came to Sausalito to visit her and she did introduce me to Sam I rationalized. After dinner, Sam played his guitar and we all sang. After a couple of glasses of wine, we thought we sounded like a real band.

Sam and I spent the remainder of my vacation together with the exception of the time he was in school. "Don't you have to study for your classes?" I asked.

"Yes, but I can manage this week with doing the minimum required. Besides I have a friend that knows the teacher." I threw a pillow at him and he tackled me to the floor. Laughing, we soon were in each other's arms.

"Where is this going?" Sam was the first to broach the subject we had been dancing around.

"I don't know," I said. "I do know that I am crazy about you which is nuts since we just met a few days ago. You are everything I've wanted in a partner and was afraid to find. Then we have the issue of us living in two different places."

"I know and I honestly don't know what do to about that." Neither one of us was ready to have a serious discussion.

"Can we enjoy today and see what happens in the future?"

"Sure," Sam said in agreement.

# Chapter Seven

It was ten o'clock Sunday morning and time for me to return to Sacramento. I was packed and waiting for Sam. He had asked to take me to the airport and Gretchen graciously understood and said yes. My flight left at two in the afternoon and I needed to be at the airport by noon. Sam arrived a few minutes before ten o'clock, put my luggage in the Jeep and I said goodbye to Gretchen promising to call her when I got home.

Sam and I were quiet on the way to the airport. We got there at eleven which gave us a final hour together. Sam parked the Jeep. I checked my luggage and we walked around the terminal. We finally found an empty row of seats and sat down. Sam took ahold of my hand and we looked at each other. In unison Sam said, "Can I come to see you" and I said "Will you come to see me." We laughed and both said 'yes.' At least the tension was broken.

"Sam, I can't tell you what a wonderful week this has been for me."

"I feel the same way and want to kidnap you and keep you here with me."

"That would get you in a lot of trouble. The flight from San Francisco to Sacramento is short and doesn't cost that much. We can see each other on weekends. When you get out of school, we can have more time together."

"I know and it's all the more reason for me to graduate early."

"I can come to San Francisco on weekends. I am sure Gretchen won't mind."

"You could always stay with me. My roommate informed me last night that he was moving, so I have the place to myself."

"Now that is convenient! When can I come?"

"Sweetheart, you can come anytime, day or night."

Just then they called my flight and I still needed to get through security. "I gotta run or I'll miss my flight."

"Not without a hug and kiss," Sam said taking me in his arms.

"I'll call when I get home."

"And I'll miss you," Sam whispered in my ear as I turned to run to my gate.

I got home late in the afternoon, unpacked and called Gretchen knowing I would be on the phone for a while with Sam. I poured a glass of wine, hit speed call and Sam answered on the second ring.

"Do you miss me yet?" I asked.

"What do you think? When you aren't here, I feel this empty place in my heart."

"How sweet. When do you think you can come to Sacramento for a visit?

"If that is an invitation, I will be there Friday evening."

We talked for another hour. I was exhausted and knew I would have a pile of work on my desk in the morning. For some reason, I really didn't care. Despite being tired, I didn't get to bed until nearly midnight. Just as I crawled under the covers, the phone rang. Looking at caller ID, I saw it was Sam. "I just thought I would call and tell you I miss you." I smiled and told Sam I missed him too and we hung up.

# Chapter Eight

I got up after my usual four hours of sleep and was at the office at six o'clock the following morning. I stopped at the corner Starbuck's and got a latte and croissant. As I suspected, my desk was stacked with files that needed attention. I quickly went through my existing files to see if anything was urgent. Thankfully, there wasn't. My next task was to tackle the new files. As I was going through the cases and putting them in like stacks, my boss came in.

"Welcome back, Julie. How was San Francisco?"

"Great. It looks like it was busy here."

"Yes, it was and there are a couple of files we need to address. Take the morning and get acquainted with the cases on your desk and let's meet after lunch this afternoon."

"Thanks, John."

"By the way, San Francisco must have been good for you. You look marvelous."

Blushing, I didn't say anything and John left my office.

My new cases included a wife beating, failure to pay alimony, failure to show up for final divorce proceedings, and another five cases. I met with John in the afternoon and we strategized how to proceed. I had not been made partner with the firm, so John tended to watch over me. I didn't mind. John always meant well and was a good teacher.

"We have a new case that is rather complicated and wondered

if you would like to work on it with Casey. I am afraid it is going to require working a couple of weekends, to include this weekend."

I didn't know what to say. Sam was coming and I wanted to see him. On the other hand, this was an important rape case and I needed the experience and exposure in court.

Sam called me that evening, as I knew he would. I explained the offer from John and Sam said he understood and would only miss me more. In all honesty, I was also concerned about our sleeping arrangements when Sam came. We are adults and this should not be an issue. Yet, it needed to be talked about before Sam came. Was I ready to sleep with him? I honestly didn't know. Did I love him? I honestly wasn't sure. I had some deep feelings for Sam and loved being with him. However, I was also on vacation and things might be different when he was in my environment. Why does life and love need to be so complicated?

Work kept me busy and I put in sixty hours the first week. In addition, I met with the team of attorneys on the weekend who were assigned to the rape, murder and suicide case.

I missed Sam terribly, especially in the evenings. When I should have been reviewing cases, we were talking on the phone. He got several new gigs and school was going well. He still planned to graduate in November, just four months away.

"Can you come to Sacramento this weekend?"

"I can, Julie, but not until Saturday morning. I have a gig on Friday night."

I was disappointed, but Sam had understood when I had to work the prior weekend. "That would be marvelous. What flight are you taking?"

"The first flight out and I'll be the first one off the plane."

# Chapter Nine

I drove to the airport Saturday morning feeling like a young girl with her first love. I couldn't wait to see Sam. His plane was getting in at ten o'clock and I had plenty of time. It was raining hard and the streets were wet and slippery. Suddenly a large SUV swerved in front of me and I hit it broadside. I heard the crunch of metal and plastic and then I was unconscious.

When I woke up, I heard beeping noises, my left arm was tied to a board and there were people running around in blue outfits. "Julie," I heard a familiar voice.

"Sam?" I said in a fog.

"Julie," I heard that voice again and through blurred vision recognized Sam.

"Where am I?"

"You are in the hospital in the Intensive Care Unit.

"Why, what happened?"

"You were on the way to the airport to pick me up and a car swerved in front of you."

"What's wrong with me? I hurt so badly."

"Sweetheart, you have a broken arm and leg, a ruptured spleen, a concussion and multiple contusions. The doctors had to take you to surgery and they took out your spleen."

"That can't be possible, can it?

"I am afraid so."

"How did you find me?"

"It wasn't as romantic as Carey Grant finding Debra Kerr in A Love Affair to Remember."

"Really?" I laughed and wished I hadn't.

"When you weren't at the airport, I knew something must be wrong. I took a taxi to your condo and a neighbor told me about the accident and that you were in the hospital. With all of the HIPPA laws, I had to tell them I was your fiancé before they would let me in to see you."

"I always knew you would be there to look after me. What day is it?"

"This is Tuesday."

"Tuesday, what about school."

"Remember, I have connections with the teacher."

"Oh My Gosh, I have files that need to be attended to at work."

"I met your boss, John, yesterday and he told me to tell you that he has assigned your files to other attorneys in the office and not to worry."

"Not to worry. What if I lose my job?"

"You aren't going to lose your job, young lady," John said as he entered the room.

"John, I am so sorry to put you in this predicament. Couldn't I work from home?"

"The entire office and I want you to get well before you come back to work. There will be no working from home."

"But . . ."

"There are no buts about it. Now, I've met your young man and believe you will be in good hands. I need to run and I'll stop by later." He shook Sam's hand and left.

"When can I go home? Oh, wait. Am I going to need someone to take care of me?"

"Sweetheart, you have someone who will be with you until you are up and on your own."

"Who would that be?"

"Me. Who else?"

Sam had taken a leave from school. He would not take no for an answer.

Since I was now awake, I was transferred out of the ICU to a private room. How does anyone get better with all of the noise and confusion in the ICU? I was no less happy in a private room than I was in the ICU. I begged John to give me files which he wouldn't do. Sam brought me my laptop. It was fully charged, thank you Sam. I turned it on and proceeded to check my e-mails. Responding to my messages was another matter because the cast on my right arm extended to my fingers. I was right-handed and couldn't type with my left hand. In desperation, I slammed, my laptop closed. "Sam, get me out of here."

When the doctor came in that evening making his rounds, I was sitting up in bed and made every effort to look like I hadn't spent the past five days in the hospital. "Dr. Henry, please let me go home."

"Well, Julie, you are doing very well. Do you have someone who can stay with you for a while? You are going to need help and you can't drive."

Sam was with me in the room. "Doctor, I can stay as long as Julie needs me."

"Very well, Sam. Julie I'll discharge you and you may go home in the morning. I'll see you in my office next Monday. Sam, you'll need to pick up Julie's prescriptions before she goes home. Julie, if you are in pain, I want you to take your pain medication. You had a nasty accident and were tossed around in your car despite the seat belt you were wearing. In fact, without that seat belt, you may not be with us today."

Dr. Henry left and Sam had my prescription slips in his hand. "Was the accident that bad?"

"Yes, it was. Your car was totally destroyed and the paramedics had to get you out with the Jaws of Life."

My life suddenly took on a new meaning. At the age of twenty-eight I was nearly a fatal accident victim. I looked at Sam and extended my hand. Sam took my hand and sat down beside me. "I am sorry I've been such a bitch."

"You're not a bitch. A little cranky and demanding, but not a bitch. I am going to go home and make sure you have everything you need. It's getting late and the nurses are going to kick me out anyway."

"What do you mean, they are going to kick you out? You have been sleeping in that miserable recliner every night. Go home and get a good night's sleep. You'll need that rest when I get home."

"Yes, mam!"

The nurses put me back to bed. They told me my discharge orders had been written and I could leave in the morning when Sam came back to pick me up. Sam was back at the hospital at seven o'clock the next morning. Because it was change of shift for the nurses, we had to wait an hour. I was getting anxious to leave and Sam had all he could do to keep me from trying to walk out. Well, that would have been difficult with one leg in a cast. Finally at eight o'clock, one of the aids came in with a wheelchair and I was wheeled out to the front entrance and into Sam's rent-a-car.

"A sedan?"

"Yep, I had to have a car and thought you would be able to get in and out better with a sedan."

"Sam, you think of everything."

"Thank you," Sam was smiling that wonderful surfer smile and I knew everything was going to be okay.

# Chapter Ten

My condo was a two-storey building with a bedroom downstairs and the master bedroom upstairs. The only way I could get up the stairs was to have an elevator, or have someone carry me. Neither option was viable. Sam had set up the bedroom downstairs and moved the furniture so that I had a clear path between the bedroom, kitchen and bathroom.

In the hospital I had sponge baths and I was dying to get into the shower. This was going to pose a problem. I couldn't take a shower and a bath was out of the question because of the casts on my arm and leg. Sam read my mind, thank you again Sam, and had put out a washcloth, towel and bar of soap on the edge of the bathtub.

"What clothes would you like from the closet?"

"There should be a set of sweats on the right-hand side."

"Found them," Sam said walking back into the bathroom.

I was fussing with my hair and muttering that it felt dirty. "Say, I have an idea. Why don't I wash your hair?"

I looked up at Sam in disbelief. "You're going to wash my hair? How?"

"Well now, if you can hold your head over the side of the tub, I can use your hand-held shower head, suds you up and whoa lah! You will have clean hair."

"Are you serious?"

"Of course. Didn't I tell you I went to Lady Hair Washing School

Over a Tub?" Sam had the towel draped over his arm and wheeled me to the side of the tub. I started laughing and Sam maintained his composure as he suds and rinsed my hair..

"Madame, if you will please bend over so zee head is over zee tub, we will proceed." I did as I was told, the warm water running through my hair.

"That feels like heaven," I said to no one in particular. Suddenly, the water was running down my back and onto the floor.

"Oops! If Madame pleases, zee water must stay in zee hair."

I started laughing and Sam broke character and laughed with me. He rinsed my hair and started towel drying it.

"Sam, you are the best. Now, scram while I bathe the best I can and put on some real clothes."

"Call me if you need anything, like washing your back." With that I threw the wet washcloth at him. "Scram."

I found that I was soon tired and wanted nothing more than to go to bed early in my own bed. Sam insisted on sleeping in the chair next to the bed in case I needed anything. "Sam, please sleep in the bed with me. Nothing is going to happen with a cast on my arm and leg and an incision in my belly." Sam was only too happy to comply. That first night I lay in his arms and felt secure. He quickly fell asleep and thoughts running through my head kept me awake longer. Finally, I dozed off into a fitful sleep and dreamt of crashing vehicles and being locked in a car with rain coming down. I could see people outside the car looking in, but they couldn't see me. I woke up with a start and found Sam asleep next to me. It was then that I knew I was I love with him. I closed my eyes and went back to sleep snuggled next to Sam.

Sam and I had an adjustment period living together. I wasn't used to a roommate, let alone having to rely on someone. The week after my casts came off, I started physical therapy. John gave in to my insistence for working at home and brought me a couple of files. Sam made several day trips back to San Francisco to pick up his Jeep and bring back more of his belongings. He made some musical contacts in Sacramento and got a few gigs. He was happier when he was playing and singing.

One day, he came home with a grin on his face. "What's up with that big smile?"

"I stopped by the university to find out about their journalism program. Julie, I can transfer to Sacramento State without losing any credits and graduate in a semester. Classes start on Wednesday."

"That's wonderful, Sam. Uh, we need to talk about a few things, like are you moving to Sacramento and living arrangements."

"Julie, I'm sorry if I went about this backwards. We've been living together in your condo for the past six weeks and I couldn't be happier. I didn't think I could leave the city, but now it doesn't make any difference. What I'm trying to say is that I love you and would fly to the moon to be with you. I'm getting gigs now in Sacramento and can finish my schooling here. You are ready to be living alone again and I can find a place nearby.

Tears were welling up in my eyes. "What's the matter, sweetheart?" he said.

"You just summed up my feelings. Sam, I realized I was in love with you the first night you brought me home from the hospital. I didn't say anything because I thought it was too early. I wanted you to move to Sacramento, but not until you got your degree."

Sam was at my side in an instant and I was in his arms. "You are already settled in my condo and I see no reason for you to look for another place to live."

So, Sam officially moved in with me. He enrolled in his last classes, moved out of his home in San Francisco and I went back to work. Life was good.

We lived in my 1,200 square foot condo making adjustments over the next few months. With Christmas around the corner, I wondered how we would accommodate a Christmas tree.

"What did you do in the past?" Sam asked.

"I haven't had a Christmas tree in so many years I've forgotten what it is like to have one."

"That will change this year. I wouldn't know how to celebrate Christmas without a tree."

We went Christmas tree shopping in December and bought decorations together. I felt we were starting our own holiday tradition and it felt wonderful.

Holiday party invitations began arriving and we were invited as a couple. We relished in the holiday activities knowing that if we were not together, we would either be attending events alone, or not at all. One evening we were attending a gala sponsored by my law firm. I had purchased an evening gown, a sapphire blue that set off my blue eyes and dark hair. Sam had on a tuxedo and was obviously uncomfortable in it. Just as I was finishing getting dressed, Sam walked in. "Jule, you look absolutely beautiful. If we weren't' already dressed, I'd have you in bed and making love to you."

"What's to stop you?"

Sam started taking off his bowtie. "No, Sam. I was only kidding."

"Okay, I can wait for tonight."

"By the way, you look good enough to eat," I said putting my arms around his neck.

"Enough, or we will stay home and this is an important party for you, sweetheart."

And so, we went through the holidays with one party after another. Those who had not seen me in a while, congratulated us on our relationship. We were both beaming and Sam was proudly at my side.

# Chapter Eleven

Sam finished his course work, graduated with a degree in Journalism and started his internship with the Sacramento Daily Courier. My law firm won our big rape, murder and suicide case and we were awarded a huge sum of money.

Sam insisted we go out to dinner to celebrate our successes and it was Valentine's Day. We had both been working too many hours and it was time to reconnect. There was an elegant and expensive restaurant by the State Capital that I had always wanted to try. Sam made reservations and we gussied up for the evening. Taking the elevator to the restaurant on the twentieth floor, we held hands and didn't need to say anything. I was so very happy and content. What more could I ask for? I was alive and with the love of my life.

Dinner was fabulous and we had a view of the city and Capital. "Sam, you out did yourself tonight."

"I hope so, because there's more."

"What could be more?"

"Well, I have something for you." Sam took out a small box from is coat pocket. Could it be? I thought. Sam sat the box down on the table, got out of his chair and knelt down on one knee beside me. "Julie, I love you more than anything and can't even imagine life without you. Would you marry me?" The entire restaurant was watching us and began to applaud.

I could feel tears welling up in my eyes again. I smiled at Sam and felt only love in my heart. "Sam, of course I will marry you. I've been in love with you since we first met in San Francisco. So, what's in the box?"

"I almost forgot." Sam picked up the box and opened it. He placed a solitaire engagement ring on my finger. It was beautiful and exactly what I would have picked out. We got another round of applause before Sam kissed me and returned to his seat.

Leaving the restaurant, we decided to walk the block to the Capital. It was a marvelous evening with a chill in the air. I had progressed well with my physical therapy so the walk was therapeutic for my leg. We walked hand in hand and had no need for conversation.

"Let's sit over there on the bench," Sam suggested.

"Sam, about our wedding. Considering your family and how many friends you have in San Diego, I think we should get married there."

"Sweetheart, I am so glad to hear that because that is exactly where I would like to get married. Have you been to San Diego before?"

"Just once a long, long time ago. What do you have in mind?"

"There are so many places that are appropriate. We could do a chapel or beach wedding. Balboa Park is a favorite place of a lot of couples. What I'd really like to do is take a trip to San Diego in the next few weeks. I want you to meet my parents and family. I've told them about you and they are anxious to meet you. We can take a couple of days to look around and decide on a spot for the wedding."

"You are so considerate. You know I've not seen my dad in years. I wonder if he would like to give me away."

"Sweetie, you're his only child and daughter. I'm sure he'll be delighted to give you away. Why don't you call him?"

To change the subject, I asked, "When would you like to get married?" I was sure Sam had thought of dates. After all, he had made plans to ask me to marry him, so he had a heads up.

Sam was quiet. Perhaps he hadn't thought of wedding dates.

"I have an idea. My head is swimming right now. Let's look at places first and find out what is available and then we can decide on a date."

Sam gave me a hug and a kiss, "Perfect."

"Then there is the invitation list, reception, band, food . . ."

"Hold on, now my head is swimming. How about we go home and get in some snuggling and loving."

"Works for me.

# Chapter Twelve

We made plans to go to San Diego on Friday the first weekend of March. We both got off early from work for our two o'clock flight. Sam's parents were delighted we were coming and insisted that we stay with them. We flew into the San Diego Airport and arrived at four in the afternoon. Sam's parents met us outside the security area. I would have no problem recognizing his father. Sam looked just like him, minus the grey hair and a few wrinkles.

"Mom and Dad, thanks for meeting us." Sam put his arm around my waist. "This is Julie. Julie, this is my mother, Sara, and my dad, Corey." His parents looked like people I would like. "I'm so pleased to meet you both," I said as I extended my hand in a handshake. "Julie, how wonderful to meet you," Sara said as she ignored my hand and gave me a big hug. Corey followed behind his wife and gave me a hug. I've never felt so welcomed by strangers in all of my life.

We walked to the baggage area and waited for our luggage. Sam fought the crowds to claim our two suitcases leaving me with his parents. Normally, I would have been uncomfortable with people I had just met. However, Sara and Corey made everything so easy. Our suitcases were at the front of the luggage carrier and we exited the building. The weather was beyond perfect. The traffic out of the parking lot was less than perfect and we sat in line to pay our ticket for twenty minutes. Once we were on the freeway, Sam and

I snuggled close to each other in the back seat.

"What part of San Diego do you live in?" I asked not having a clue which direction we were headed.

"We are not far from the airport and should be home soon." Sara continued, "We own a historical house in Point Loma. Corey and I bought the house soon after we were married. We really couldn't afford it, but I was so in love with the house that Corey agreed to buy it. Now, forty years later, we still love it. You know we raised six kids there, so there are a lot of memories."

"Sam tells me that you are both doctors."

"Yes, I am a pediatrician and Corey is a heart surgeon."

That explains the money.

"We have a hectic family and cherish the time we can get together. Of our six children, four are doctors. Sally, our youngest is still in school at UCSD studying art and music. Sam, of course finally finished his college course work. We told the children when they were very young that we would pay for their education and lodging with an allowance until they were thirty years old. Sam just finished under the line." This amused Sam and his parents. And, that explains the Jeep and apartment on the Presidio.

We were driving through one of the most beautifully kept neighborhoods I had ever seen. All of the homes appeared to be historical houses from the 1930's and 1940's and were so California. We came to a gated home and Corey punched in a code. I was in awe having come from a middle-class family. The grounds were immaculate and the house a Spanish style home. I was waiting for the butler to appear, but that did not happen. "We're here, sweetheart."

"Are you sure this is the right place?"

Sam laughed, "Yes, it is. Come on and meet the rest of the family."

Just then what seemed like a small crowd came out of the house. Everyone was talking at the same time and giving hugs. I got caught up in the crowd and loved it. Soon Sam and I were laughing.

I was introduced to the eldest son, Mathew and his wife. They were followed by Mark and his wife. I met number three and four sons and their lovely wives. And last was Amy, the youngest at the age of twenty. She was beautiful and I could see her mother in her. This is where Sam gets his connectivity and ability to love completely. There was so much love in this family I could feel it.

"Is this all there is?" I asked Sam. "Oh, no. You still have to meet the kids who are in the pool." The kids were all over the place and the yelling was incredible. "We let them get crazy because they fall asleep early and the adults have some quiet time."

The maid showed us to our room. I was pleased that Sam's parents were okay with us sharing a bedroom and we didn't have to do any explaining. Even though we were engaged and living together, I didn't know how they felt about this arrangement.

It was five o'clock and Sam suggested we walk to the beach. "What about your family?" I asked. "My parents will be busy taking calls from the hospital and so will my brothers. Their wives will take care of the kids. Besides, I want to show you where I grew up."

We changed clothes and headed to the beach. "I had forgotten how different the beaches are here from northern California. It's flat without cliffs."

"We have cliffs here, but you're right, the beaches are very different. Pacific Beach, Ocean Beach and some of the beaches of La Jolla are flat and sandy. Let's take a walk on the beach. You might want to roll up your pants and take off your sandals." Sam was rolling up his pants and his shoes were off in an instant.

We walked along the sand and the waves teased us with their songs of softness and tenderness. I was feeling very sentimental and Sam picked up on it. "Are you okay, sweetheart?"

"Yes," I said as I stopped and put my arms around Sam. "Do you know how lucky you are to have such a wonderful family?"

"Yes, Julie, I do. I thought about this before we came and decided that I had no control over who my family is, just as you have no control over who your family is. In a way you were abandoned when your parents got divorced and then when your mother died. I want you to know that my family will accept you as one of their own. All you have to do is love them."

"Thank you, Sam. I love you so much and will love your family also."

Sam and I were up early on Saturday and went for a run on the beach. At breakfast, Sam announced we were going wedding location hunting. His parents knew we wanted to do this excursion alone and his dad told us to take his Mercedes. We left after breakfast, put down the top of the car and took off to explore San Diego.

Sam had a list of places he wanted to visit. First on the list was Balboa Park. Here we could have an outdoor wedding. "With a little pull from my dad, we could be married in the San Diego Zoo among the animals."

"Really?" I looked at him with disbelief.

"Well, it's an option," Sam laughed.

Next, we went to Pacific Beach and visited a chapel overlooking the ocean. It was nice, but not big enough for Sam's family and their friends. From there we went to La Jolla which was beautiful but I didn't see any place that excited me. After driving around the city all morning, Sam suggested we go to the San Diego pier for lunch. The pier housed an uncountable number of huge yachts. I'm not sure I had ever seen so much money in one place.

We parked the car and walked to the restaurant in the yacht club and waited to be seated outside. "Tell me your family owns a yacht."

"As a matter of fact, they do. See that sixty-foot yacht at the end of the pier?"

"Yes."

"That is the Sara-Corey and belongs to our family."

"My goodness, are there any other surprises you have for me?"

"Nope."

We were seated and the waitress called Sam by name and took

our order. "You know Sam, one of the things I love about you is how you don't flaunt what your family has. When I met you, I assumed you were a struggling singer and guitar player in San Francisco. Then I find that you lived at the Presidio and drove a new Jeep. How do you keep from being stuck up?"

Sam laughed and took my hand. "Julie, both of my parents came from poor families. They went to school on scholarships to Stanford University and they met each other their second year of medical school. As they tell us, they lived in a low rent apartment and had second jobs to make ends meet. They both so believe in providing care to those who depend upon them, they would have continued their way of living forever. However, fate has a way of paying back and they became very successful physicians. When they bought the house I grew up in, they knew it was a good house to raise a family. Of course, my mother loves children being a pediatrician and my father spends most of his practice taking care of people at the other end of the spectrum, the elderly. They instilled their good morals on us kids and expect we will do the same with our children. Am I grateful? Yes, every day and you are going to be a part of this wonderful family."

I had nothing to say. I took Sam's hand and rested my head on his shoulder looking out at the ocean. Sam what is that?" I referred to the jumping objects from the ocean. "Those, my love, are dolphins and if you listen carefully, you can hear their love calls."

When I heard the dolphins making their love calls, I knew why I had met a guitar player and singer from San Francisco.

We sat quietly until our meal arrived. Suddenly, I had a thought I had to share with Sam immediately. "Sam, what would you say to us getting married on your family yacht?" I was so excited, I kept on talking. "We could have the captain marry us, your family could be in attendance and we could invite your friends to the reception. I want a formal wedding, but I don't want a large wedding. We could have both. What do you think?"

"Jule, I love you. What a marvelous idea. I have a lot of friends, but honestly, they would rather be invited to a fun reception than to dress up for a wedding. Let's talk with my parents when we get back."

"Sam, I need to talk to you about something. Traditionally the bride's family pays for the wedding and you know my dad has no money. I would like to use the bonus money I got from that big settlement the firm got."

"Sweetheart, my parents have already told me that they want to pay for this wedding. I think it has to do with my mother wanting to be a part of the planning. The first four weddings were done by my brother's wives."

"Then she shall be part of the planning every step of the way."

Sam's parents loved the idea of a wedding on the yacht. Sara began making up the guest list and designing the invitations. She was having so much fun that I let her take the lead. Later that day, she gave me a list of florists she knew that could provide flowers. "Sara, would you mind picking out the flowers? As long as I have red and white roses, I will be happy." As Sara made her extensive lists of things to do, Corey asked us what date we were getting married. Sam and I looked at each other and laughed. We had forgotten that important part of the wedding. "How about Julie and I get back to you on that?" Sam said.

# Chapter Thirteen

When Sam and I returned from San Diego, we immediately got caught up in our work. I had five more cases than the norm. Sam had finished his internship and was now working as a journalist for the newspaper. When Sam had evening or night gigs, I would go with him when I had time.

One evening mid-May Sara, Sam's mother, called. Sam answered his cell phone and I could hear him talking to his mother. "No, we haven't set a date for the wedding. Yes, I know the invitations need to be sent out. I will talk with Julie and get back to you in a few days. I love you too, Mom."

"Jule, we need to set our wedding date."

"I know, I heard your end of the conversation with your mother. When would be the slowest time of the year at the newspaper?"

"I honestly don't know. I doubt there is any slow time. How about you?"

"Do you know what I would really want?"

"What would that be, sweetheart?"

I walked over to Sam and sat down beside him. "I would love a Valentine's Day wedding on the Yacht. We could have a valentine theme and our colors could be red and white."

"Actually, I like the idea and we have almost a year to make plans. That would take some stress off of my mom and we would be able to give the newspaper and your firm enough time to anticipate our leave."

"Why don't you call your mom back?"

"I'll let you do that. She'll ask me all sorts of questions about colors, the cake and other stuff I can't answer."

I called Sara and she answered on the second ring. It must be that doctor on call instinct to always pick up the phone. "Hi Sara, its Julie. I am sorry Sam and I didn't get back to you on the wedding date, but we talked and would like to get married on Valentine's Day."

Before I could say anything else, I heard Sara exclaim what a marvelous idea that would be. "The entire family will be here and the weather is usually beautiful that time of the year. We could have the wedding at two o'clock with a four o'clock reception. Would that work for you and Sam? Oh, and how about colors? Have you thought about what colors you want? Something in red would be nice."

"Whoa, Sara. You're going too fast for me." I could see Sam out of the corner of my eye smiling. "Sam how about a two o'clock wedding?" He raised his hand and gave me a thumbs up. "Sara, two o'clock would be a perfect time for the wedding. And, yes, we have decided on colors. They should be red and white with red and white roses." Sara asked if we were coming to San Diego anytime soon so we could talk about the wedding in more detail. I conferred with Sam and told Sara we could be in San Diego in two weeks.

"Jule, you still haven't called your father."

"I know."

"Why don't you call him right now? It isn't going to get any easier and I'll bet you a quart of Hagen Dazs ice cream he will be delighted you called."

"For a quart of Hagen Dazs, you are on. Okay, here goes." I punched in my dad's number on my cell phone. It rang five times and I was ready to hand up when he answered. "Hi, Dad."

"Julie, how wonderful to hear from you. How have you been? It has been too long since you called. How was your trip to Sausalito?"

I filled dad in on my work schedule and when it came to my trip to Sausalito, I told him about Sam. He was glad that I had met someone. Then I told him about my accident. "Why didn't you call me?" he asked. I told him there wasn't anything he could do and that Sam stayed with me the entire time. "Dad, Sam and I are getting married on Valentine's Day in San Diego. I would like for you to give me away." My last statement was with a timid voice because I was unsure if my dad would even attend our wedding.

"Julie, how wonderful for you and Sam. Yes, I would love to give you away. After all, you are my only daughter. Are we going to get to meet this Sam anytime soon?"

"Of course, Dad. We'll be in San Diego in a couple of weeks. Perhaps we can meet you and Terry somewhere between there and Los Angeles for lunch."

"Just let us know. I need to go now. Keep in touch."

"Well?" Sam asked. I told Sam Dad was going to give me away and would attend the wedding. "Sam when we go to San Diego, we need to meet Dad and Terry for lunch. He wants to meet you."

"Of course, Julie." Sam knew the phone conversation was difficult for me. He motioned for me to come and sit next to him on the sofa. "Sweetheart, take the talk with your dad for what it was. He didn't turn you down for the wedding. Not all families are the same. Remember how much I love you and will never leave you." I looked up at Sam with tears in my eyes. "Thank you Sam, I love you so much."

# Chapter Fourteen

While we were in San Diego, Sam and I made plans to meet my dad and Terry at a restaurant in Newport Beach. The restaurant was on the beach front and for a Monday was not particularly busy. "Are you nervous?" Sam asked. I simply nodded my head and shuffled my feet. "When was the last time you saw your dad and Terry?" I murmured that it had been a couple of years. I looked up and saw Dad and Terry walking towards us.

"Dad, how wonderful to see you," I said giving him a hug and kiss on the cheek. "Terry, it is good to see you again," I added. Introductions were made and I was holding onto Sam's hand so tightly I could almost see him wince. "Well, let's go in and have lunch. We made reservations for a window table."

Lunch was a polite affair. We talked a bit about the wedding and how we met. Dad asked about the accident and my recovery. Two hours later, Sam paid the bill and we left the restaurant. "Honey, keep in touch. Sam it was good to meet you." Dad and Sam shook hands and we walked to our car.

"You and your dad didn't talk about his being in the wedding."

"I know. We will later."

"Come on, let's go walk on the beach. That will bring back that smile I love so much." We took off our shoes, Sam took my hand and we ran down to the beach. Sam was right, my smile did come back.

The summer flew by. We made a couple of trips to San Diego so

Sara and I could finalize the wedding plans. The reception invitation list grew from one hundred to three hundred. "How do you know so many people?" I asked Sam.

"Only a few are my friends, the rest are mom and dad's friends. Remember, they have lived here their entire married and working life."

I left the food up to Sara for the wedding. Corey found a captain to officiate at the ceremony. My maids of honor were Gretchen (of course) and Sam's younger sister Amy. Sara also took care of the maid of honor dresses which were red velvet with white fur trim. My dress was made in San Diego by a friend of Sara's. Despite my wish to have a traditional wedding, I realized I could have any dress design I wanted. With Sara's help, I choose a white velvet wedding dress with white fur and a long train. I would wear red and white roses intertwined in my dark, long hair. Through Sam's contacts in Sacramento, he found a band in San Diego consisting of a guitar player and a piano player with a fellow on saxophone. The only stipulation was that they play folk music in between requests. I hoped Sara and I had thought of everything.

When we were making our wedding plans, I asked Sam if he wanted me to take his last name. "Why?" he said. "You are known professionally by your last name." I was delighted with Sam's insight. I have never understood why women have to change their name and men get to keep their names for a lifetime.

Sam and I both took a month off from work for our wedding and honeymoon. We flew down to San Diego a week before the wedding. I thought seven days might be too much time. To the contrary, Sara and I were busy every day. If Sara was tied up with her practice at the hospital, one of her daughter-in-law's filled in. Gretchen came down four days in advance and had the final fitting for her dress.

Suddenly, it was February 14th and Sam and I were about to be wed. Corey had washed the yacht top to bottom and decorated it with hearts. The ceremony was scheduled for two o'clock.

Gretchen, Amy and I had an appointment with Sara's hair dresser at nine o'clock. We also had pedicures and manicures. After our hair was done, the makeup artist came to the house. I have never been pampered so much and Sam's parents were paying for all of the wedding activities.

I didn't see Sam all morning. I assumed he was drinking Bloody Marys' and playing pool to pass the time away. After all, he only needed to put on his tuxedo.

It was noon and I was ready to put on my wedding dress. I had my last fitting two days prior and loved what I saw. With makeup and my hair done up I was amazed at how pretty I looked. My white velvet dress with its white fur trim fit like a glove. At one o'clock a limousine drove up to the house to take the bride's side of the wedding party to the yacht club. Sara had insisted on the traditional belief that the groom should not see the bride prior to the wedding. Although I thought it was a little silly, I was willing to go along with her whim. The limousine felt a bit empty with only myself, Gretchen, Amy, Sara and our flower girls.

When we drove up to the dock, I couldn't believe how beautiful the yacht looked. Sara and I carefully walked down the dock to the yacht. Crew members helped us onto the deck and escorted us to the stateroom. Once in the stateroom, we were offered glasses of champagne. I was ever so grateful for the alcohol to sooth my nerves.

It was time for the ceremony to begin. At two o'clock the band started to play 'The Wedding Song' by Peter, Paul and Mary. The door to the stateroom opened and Gretchen and Amy began the wedding procession. My father, offered his arm to me. I took a deep breath, took my father's arm and walked the short distance to the deck.

Sam was waiting for me. He was so handsome in his black tuxedo, red cummerbund and bowtie. He smiled at me with his surfer smile and I felt his love. When I met up with Sam, my father left my side and I was standing next to Sam. We waited until the Wedding Song was finished relishing in the meaning of the words.

The captain instructed the guests to be seated. Sam and I had written our vows and the captain instructed us to recite the first words together.

> We met unexpectedly, our love came quickly.
> We walked on the beach, stars within our reach.
> Sunrises glow with promises, sunsets fill us with memories.
> Dolphins sing their love songs and devotion fills the skies.
> You are the love I hoped to find, the
> one to live with for a life time.
> Our destiny is to be as one, for today
> and always my loved one.
> I Julie, take you Sam as my lifelong love
> and partner for now and forever to cherish
> and to love until death do us part.
> I Sam, take you Julie as my lifelong love
> and partner for now and forever to cherish
> and to love until death do us part.

We exchanged wedding bands and the captain pronounced us husband and wife followed by a round of applause. Sam and I kissed and then turned to face our family. My father was seated with Terry and he gave me a smile and a wink.

The band began to play and Sam and I walked off of the yacht to the limousine. We didn't have far to go because the reception was at the yacht club and we were taken to a private room so we could regroup before the endless photos were taken.

"I can't call you a Mrs., but I can certainly call you my wife."

"That is the most wonderful sound in the world. I love you, Sam."

"And I love you, Jule."

We had little time to ourselves before the photographer began setting up for photographs. We posed in front of and on top of the baby grand piano. We went outside for pictures with the bay in the background, we had pictures on the yacht and others that soon became a blur. When we got the first round of proofs, we couldn't remember many of them being taken.

At four o'clock, the reception began and the guests began to arrive. Sara had outdone herself with the appetizers and endless champagne. The kids loved the chocolate fountain and the adults loved the open bar.

Once again, I was barraged with the names and faces of Sam's longtime friends. Sara and Corey introduced their friends and I soon gave up on trying to remember any names. Sam and I had opted out of the traditional receiving line. I wanted to enjoy my wedding, not stand in line and shake three hundred hands.

At five o'clock dinner was served. Sam and I along with the wedding party were at the head table and we were served first. Both Sam and I were so hyped up that we barely ate which was unfortunate because Sara had arranged for Filet Mignon and Lobster.

With dinner over and the dishes being retrieved by the wait persons, the band started playing with the first song reserved for the bride and groom. True to tradition, my father asked for my hand. We walked out on to the dance floor, he held my hand and with the other hand placed it on my back and we began to dance. It was the first time I had ever danced with my father. "Honey, you look beautiful and I am so proud of you." I was taken aback by his comment and it brought tears to my eyes. "Thank you, Dad, I love you." Sam cut in and we took off in a whirlwind of dance and love.

By nine o'clock I had my shoes off and Sam had taken off his tie. We were both exhausted and still needed to change clothes and go to the hotel. Sam and I excused ourselves and retired to our room where we quickly changed clothes. Many of the guests had left because of the late hour. When I threw my bouquet, it was caught by Gretchen and we exchanged a girlfriend secret smile. Sam and I ran to the limousine and we were whisked off to the

Westin Hotel in the Gaslamp District.

The hotel clerk at the front desk was expecting us and the bellhop escorted us to the honeymoon suite overlooking the bay. "I'm so tired I could crash," I said out loud to anyone who would listen to me. "Me too." Sam chimed in. "Look at the champagne and fruit basket. Care for anything?"

"Just you. I am going to change clothes one more time tonight." Our bags had been delivered to the hotel room earlier. When I went into the bathroom, there was a white lace negligee and robe hanging from the shower rod. There was a note from Sara and Corey. "Welcome to our family. May you and Sam share the love and years we have had together. You have quickly become very special to us and we love you."

I put on the negligee and robe and found Sam on the patio off of our room. "Sam, you have to read this from your parents." Sam read the note, took me in his arms and said, "Let's always share our love and years starting tonight." He picked me up and carried me to bed where we made love for the first time as husband and wife.

# Chapter Fifteen

Our flight to Hawaii wasn't until two o'clock the next afternoon. I slept in and when I woke up, I found Sam sitting in front of the glass door leading to the balcony. I stretched and put on my new lace negligee and robe.

"Hey, sleepy head. How about some coffee and breakfast?"

"That sounds great, but I'm not ready to get dressed yet."

"Then follow me to the balcony. This is my own very special honeymoon restaurant complete with fresh coffee and breakfast."

"You ordered breakfast?"

"Nothing is too good for my new bride."

I leaned down and kissed Sam as he got up and we went outside. The San Diego Bay was magnificent at that time of the day. There were sailboats in the harbor and across the bay were several Navy ships.

We lazed around the room until it was time to get dressed and then took a taxi to the airport. The flight to Hawaii was five hours and we both slept most of the way.

We arrived at the Honolulu International Airport at six o'clock and were greeted with leis when we got off the plane. We had a short time to catch our flight to Kauai. As a wedding gift, Sam's parents had given us five nights and four days at the Marriott Kauai Beach Club. After we registered, we were escorted to our ocean side villa by gondola along the hotel's waterway system inhabited by swans that surrounded the buildings.

"Sam, I have never been so pampered in my life. How can we thank your parents?"

"Sweetheart, they know."

"Are you going to carry me across the threshold?"

"What a novel idea," Sam said as he picked me up and carried me through the door to our fabulous home for the next few days.

Sam tipped the bellhop and we explored our surroundings. We had a kitchen, sitting room, master bed room and bath complete with a sauna.

"Can we stay here forever," I said falling back on the king size bed.

Just then the phone rang and Sam answered it. "Sir, when would you like your dinner served?"

"Ah, we didn't order dinner."

"We have a pre-paid dinner order from your parents for your first night with us. When may we deliver it?"

"How about in an hour?"

"What was that all about?" I asked.

"Seems mom and dad are sending us dinner in the room. Care to freshen up? Dinner is arriving in an hour."

"Join you in the shower," I offered as I ran to the bathroom.

We ate dinner on the balcony and marveled at the ocean, palm trees and warm tropical breeze. Dinner was fabulous and we discovered how tired we were with a full stomach.

The next four days were a whirlwind. We rented a jeep and drove the island. A helicopter ride took us over lush green forests and let us down in a meadow for a couple of hours of exploring. The beaches were inviting with their warm sand and mild waves.

I asked Sam if he was going to go surfing while we were in Hawaii. "No, I don't think so. I used to be an avid surfer when I was a teenager. Then one day off the coast of La Jolla, I was involved in a nasty accident and haven't been on a surf board since."

"What happened?"

"A buddy and I were out one early morning. He fell off his board and was attacked by a shark. We weren't far from the shore which makes the shark attack so unusual. I was able to get him to shore and the paramedics were there in minutes. He lost his leg and I wasn't hurt." I knew Sam didn't want to talk about the incident any further, so I didn't push him.

We scheduled a tubing trip down through the old sugar cane fields and irrigation ditches. We were fitted with helmets and head lamps and as we floated down the waterways, our guide filled us in on the history of the sugar cane plantations.

"Wouldn't it have been wonderful to experience the sugar cane fields?" Sam questioned not expecting an answer. At the end of our trip, we were served a picnic lunch and then a 4-wheel ATV picked us and transported us back to the hotel.

We snorkeled, rented bicycles, went horseback riding and took an evening cruise. On our last night, we stayed in and had room service and watched the sun go down for the last time over the tropical waters.

"This is the end of our fairy tale honeymoon," I said nestling in Sam's arms.

"Yes, but the beginning of our lives together. Let's call it an evening. I have a need to make love to you."

# Chapter Sixteen

When Sam and I returned to Sacramento after our wedding and honeymoon, we fell into a routine, as married couples do. I was on my way to making partner and the price was long hours. Sam found he loved working for the newspaper. He was an excellent journalist and as a result, was given more complex stories to cover.

Ten months after we were married, Sam came home and told me he was asked to go overseas and cover an international story.

"Really? Where would you be going, and are you going?"

"You just asked me two questions. The assignment is in India and I would be covering a story about the impoverished people of the country."

"Would you go alone?"

"No, David Ortiz, our photographer, would also be going."

"Now for my other question. Are you going?"

"Jule, I wanted to talk to you about it. It would be a great opportunity for me. The paper wants to do a series of global human rights stories and this could be the first of future assignments for me."

"Well, at least there are no wars going on in India. Sweetheart, if you want to take this assignment, I can't tell you not to go. How long would you be gone?"

"I'm not sure, but it looks like it might be a month or two."

"That is a long time. Can you be more specific?"

"Not right now. The offer just came up and I need to get

more information."

Sam decided to take the assignment in India. I wasn't particularly happy about him being gone for one or two months. On the other hand, if I was on a case that took me away from home, he would understand.

The day he left, we met David at the airport. "Please be careful," I told Sam as I said goodbye at the terminal. Call and e-mail me when you can. I love you and be safe."

"I love you too, Jule. I'll let you know when I arrive in India."

The days were agonizingly long without Sam home. I found that I worked more hours and enjoyed it less. I was learning that there was no rhyme or reason to the long hours Sam and I spent working. We never really talked about having a family and now I found myself thinking of having children.

One weekend, I flew to San Diego to be with my new family. I always found Sam's parents grounding, especially his mother. Sara and I went out to lunch the day I arrived. She knew I wanted to talk and gave me space and time to bring up what was on my mind.

"Sara, what is it like having six children? Your family seems so happy."

"Julie, it doesn't matter how many children you have. It is how you love them that matters. When Corey and I found out that I was pregnant with Matthew, we were in our third year of medical school. It couldn't have happened at a worse time. I had terrible morning sickness and we were basically broke with school loans and living expenses. When I went into labor, I knew having a child would be a miraculous happening. Matthew was born twelve hours later and when the nurses put him on my chest, I knew then that I was experiencing the ultimate in love. There is no love like that of a mother."

I was thirty years old and time was running out for me to make a decision about being a mother. Without Sam to discuss my decision, I quit taking my birth control pills while he was off on assignment.

Sam called whenever he could and filled me in on what he and David found in India. "Jule, you would not believe the living conditions here. It's worse than the ghettos of Mexico. The children live on the street and many are HIV positive. It breaks my heart."

I read the articles Sam wrote for the newspaper and reviewed the film clips David captured. A month turned into another month. "Sam when do you think you will be home?"

"David and I have turned in twelve stories with a photo series. If all goes well, we should be coming home in two weeks."

"Promise?"

"Sweetheart, I miss you so much and will do my best to be home soon."

Sam kept his promise and he was home two weeks later. He had his human rights story and I do believe he would be content to let others cover issues in improvised countries in the future.

Two months after Sam returned from India, I knew I was pregnant. When I missed my period for the second month in a row, I tested myself with a home pregnancy test. It was positive. Just to make sure, I went to my gynecologist and he confirmed I was pregnant. On the way home, I stopped in at a baby shop and purchased a pair of baby booties, yellow ones. I bought flowers at the market and put the baby booties in the center of the bouquet.

"What's with the flowers? Did I forget an important date?" Sam asked when he got home from work.

"No, not really. But there is an important date in about seven months," I said smiling coyly.

"Jule, what are you trying to tell me?"

"Well, if you look closely, you'll find a pair of baby booties in the flowers."

"You're going to have a baby? No, we're going to have a baby?"

"Yep."

"Oh my gosh, am I going to be a father?"

"That's the general idea."

Sam was ecstatic and ran around the house like a little kid. We called his parents and they were delighted. It wasn't like it was their first grandchild, but it was the first grandchild we would give them.

"We need to call your dad and Terry," Sam said to me.

"I know. Perhaps tomorrow."

"Jule, you need to call your dad."

I called and was surprised when Terry answered dad's cell phone. "Hi Terry, this is Julie, is dad there?"

"No, he's not in at the moment."

"He didn't answer the phone. Is there anything wrong?"

"Julie, your father had a heart attack two days ago and is in the intensive care unit. He didn't want me to call you."

"Terry, how is he doing?"

"Not well. He has had two stints put in his heart and is scheduled for surgery tomorrow."

I told Terry I would be there as soon as possible. My boss was sympathetic and told me to take the time off I needed. Sam and I took the first flight we could get to LA. By the time we got to the hospital, dad had another heart attack and was on life support.

"Dad?" I asked as I approached his bed. He did not respond to me and his eyes were closed. He had a breathing tube in his lungs and all of the beeping monitors reminded me of when I was in the ICU after my accident.

"Honey, your dad is in a coma," the ICU nurse told me. We waited for dad's doctor to make his rounds that evening.

"Are you family?" The doctor asked when he came into dad's room.

"Yes, I am his daughter," I said.

The doctor asked us to step into the hallway and told us that dad had a massive heart attack and wasn't expected to live. He was being kept on life support until I arrived. The next forty-eight hours were hell. Dad had made a living will stating that he was not to be kept on life support. On the third day when there no signs of brain activity, all of his life support machines were turned off and my father was pronounced dead.

Sam and I stayed for the funeral. Dad didn't have many friends so it was a small service. I didn't know how to act or what to say. I wasn't close to my dad, but he was my dad. The day after the funeral, Sam and I went home.

I found the note Sara had attached to my wedding negligee and reread it.

*Welcome to our family. May you and Sam share the love and years we have had together. You have quickly become very special to us and we love you.*

I had the note framed and put on the wall in our living room for all to read and see. Sam noticed it when he got home. "What made you frame the note mom gave to you?"

"I want us to always remember the love we have and the love we can give to our children. My mother and dad lost so much when they divorced and then my dad died without knowing he would be a grandfather."

Sam took me in his arms and rocked me as I cried.

# Chapter Seventeen

I must be on be one of those fortunate women who sail through their pregnancy. I had no morning sickness to speak of and gained the recommended amount of weight. Sam commented on how radiant I looked, "All pregnant women are radiant," I replied and he made it a point to tell me that not all women were his wife.

Sam didn't take any overseas assignments during my pregnancy. We relished in talking about our little bundle and possible names. We fully understood the sex of the baby was determined at conception and it was of no benefit to want a boy or girl. When we were offered testing to determine the baby's sex, we declined.

We made the guest bedroom into a nursery with green and yellow colors. Not knowing if it was a boy or girl, we incorporated wall paintings of cars, doll houses, puppy dogs and kittens. By the eighth month, we felt we were ready for the arrival of our little one.

Two weeks before I was due, I took a leave of absence from work. When I felt my water break, I called Sam and told him not to hurry home. That was like telling a fish not to swim in water. Twelve hours later, I went into labor and Sam rushed me to the hospital. It was another twelve hours before I delivered a healthy baby girl. She was beautiful and Sam was with me through the entire delivery. It was Sam's turn to be radiant because I have never seen such a look of love than when he gazed upon our daughter for the first time.

We were home twenty-four hours later and still had not named our baby. "Sam, I would like to call our little girl Sara after your mother."

"I thought perhaps we should name her after you."

"I don't want two Julie's in the house."

In all actuality, I believe Sam was tickled to have our baby named after his mother because he didn't dispute my suggestion. Sara was elated. None of her grandchildren had been named Sara.

It became obvious very quickly that we needed more than 1,200 square feet of living space. Things were tight with me and Sam without little Sara and all of the baby equipment and clothes she required.

"Can we afford a larger house, or condo?" I questioned one night over dinner.

"I don't see how we can afford not to buy. I don't want to buy a condo because Sara will be growing and needs to have a yard to play in. Besides, what if we have another child?"

"That is a good thought. Whoa, did you say another child? I would love to give Sara a little sister or brother, but in a couple of years."

"You'll change your mind in six months, or so."

We celebrated our second anniversary. Sara was three months old and had changed our lives. She was a good baby but still needed to be attended to in the middle of the night. I went back to work when she was two months old. We found Helen, a wonderful nanny who came to the house during the day. Helen did more than care for Sara, she cleaned house, did the grocery shopping and prepared our dinner each evening.

We found a house in the suburbs of Sacramento. It was a three-bedroom house with a den we could convert into a playroom for Sara. Our little girl was growing fast and became the love of our lives. When she took her first step, we celebrated with champagne and pizza. That was the other thing that changed, we didn't go out much anymore.

"Jule, we need to go on a vacation."

"What about Sara?"

"Sara needs a vacation, too." We both laughed.

"Why don't we go to San Diego? Your parents would love to spend time with Sara and that would give us some time together."

"Do you mind if we stay with mom and dad? You know they are going to insist upon it."

"Nope. I am going to call Sara and Corey. When would you like to go?"

"Why don't you ask mom and dad when they are free, or at least semi-free?"

Sam and I took two weeks off in August and flew to San Diego. It was the first time they had seen Sara and she was now five months old. Sara and Corey met us at the airport and Sam's mom couldn't wait to hold little Sara. What a great grandmother and doctor she was.

We took Sara to the beach and she loved the water. Getting her to not roll in the sand became a daily chore. When Sara was being watched by one of our sister-in-law's, Sam and I explored the sites of San Diego. We were on the downward swing of work stress and we were not looking forward to going back to work.

One night at dinner, Corey and Sara looked at each other. We knew they had something they wanted to say and let them have the time and space to say what was on their minds.

"Sam and Julie, your mother and I have been talking and wondered if you have ever considered moving back to San Diego? We think it would be great for Sara to grow up with her cousins and of course we would love to have you closer."

"Uh, Dad, no we haven't talked about a move. We both have good jobs in Sacramento and just bought a house."

After dinner, Sam and I went for a walk on the beach. At eight o'clock it was still light and the ocean waves were soothing. "What do you think of you parent's suggestion to move to San Diego?"

"I don't know. There are a lot of things to consider like jobs, the expense of moving and then finding a place we can afford in San Diego. Housing is more expensive here."

"If we look on the positive side, Sara would have an extended family."

"Julie, you were an only child and then a child of divorce. When your mother died, I sense that you were alone in the world."

We stopped walking and sat on the beach. I picked at the sand and didn't say anything.

"Would you like to move?"

"Sam, I don't want Sara to grow up the way I did. It's too lonely. Look at the love and attention she would have here with your parents and her aunts, uncles and cousins. It seems the biggest hurdle would be to find employment."

Sam didn't say anything and after a short silence I continued, "Sam would you want to move back?"

"Jule, I love San Diego and only went to San Francisco to go to school and get my wings clipped a little. I have an idea. We are going to be here a few more days. Let's scout out the area and get a sense of jobs. Finding a place to live would not be so difficult if we were employed."

"Let's not tell your parents until we get a better sense of what we want to do."

The next morning, Matt's wife, took little Sara for the day. We had breakfast at the Beach Pub, a sort of hole in the wall from Sam's teen years. We were armed with a tablet and pen for note taking.

"Where do you want to start?" I asked.

"There are only a few local newspapers, so let's investigate those first." Our first stop was to the San Diego Daily. Sam talked to the Human Resource person. She was impressed with Sam's overseas human rights series. She wanted to see more examples of Sam's writing and he promised to send them when we returned home.

The local papers of Escondido, San Marcos, Oceanside and San Carlos had fewer opportunities and the news coverage was limited to a small geographical area. Sam left his contact information with the HR folks and they said that they would call if anything came up.

We exhausted the possibilities for Sam. It was noon and we were both starving. "Since we are up this way, let's have lunch at the Swim and Snorkel. It is on the beach and another dive from my youth."

"You and your dives," I laughed and gave Sam's arm a squeeze.

Lunch was delicious and the view of the ocean mesmerizing. We used our cell phones to connect with the internet and bring up law firms in San Diego. The total number of attorneys was overwhelming and we needed to narrow our search to family law. "Sam, I need a resume in hand before I approach a law firm and I can't do that until we get back home."

"What do you think about telling my parents that we are considering their proposal?" I agreed with Sam and we planned to talk with Sara and Corey that evening. Along the boardwalk on the way to the car, we picked up some real estate brochures.

That night at dinner, Sam opened the conversation. "Mom and Dad, Julie and I talked about your idea of us moving to San Diego and we are considering it."

"Sam, Julie, how wonderful." Sara was about to go into her usual litany of questions when Sam continued.

"We looked into positions for the newspapers in town and Julie wants to get a resume together before she approaches a law firm."

"Son, the CEO of the San Diego paper is a patient of mine and a good friend. Let me give him a call and see what he can do."

"Dad, I would like to get the job on my own. If I have trouble getting interviews or don't hear back from the newspaper HR people, I will let you know."

"The other thing to consider is the cost of moving and finding a house we can afford." I interjected.

Sara and Corey looked at each other with mischievous smiles. "Could you and Julie go back to 1,200 square feet of living?"

"I don't know," I said looking at Sam who immediately knew where his parents were going. "Of course, the guest cottage. Is anyone using it now?" Sam asked.

"No, it's empty and the three of you could live in it until you find a house you want to buy."

# Chapter Eighteen

Things were moving way too fast and it was good to get back home where we could try to look at our options objectively. Sam sent samples of his writings, columns and overseas articles to the San Diego paper. In the meantime, I worked on my resume. Larson, Thompson and Smith were the only job I had since graduating from law school. Consequently, I enhanced my involvement in the rape, murder and suicide case my law firm won.

A month after we got home, Sam got a call from the San Diego Daily newspaper HR president. She told Sam she was impressed with his work and wanted to talk with him about an executive position. Sam was so excited he couldn't sit still the entire evening. Sam flew to San Diego two days later for an interview. He expected to talk with the HR president and was surprised when they had arranged interviews with three other executives and the CEO.

When he met with the Clyde Swartz, the CEO, Clyde said, "Sam, your last name sounds familiar. Have we met before?"

"No, sir. I believe you are a patient of my father's."

"That's what it is. Well, it certainly is a pleasure to meet a son of your dad's. Don't you have a family of doctors?"

Sam had a long conversation about his family with Mr. Swartz. "Well, Sam, you've certainly made an impression on my staff and we would like to make you an offer of the president of the overseas department. We can make it financially attractive if you agree."

"May I have a couple of days to think it over and talk with my wife? This would mean a move for us from Sacramento."

"I forgot to mention that we will pay your relocating costs. Susan from HR can explain those benefits." He called Susan in and she explained relocating benefits for an executive.

Sam flew back to Sacramento that evening and when I picked him up at the airport, he was still flying high on the adrenalin of the job offer. "Jule, they offered me the position of president of the overseas department and I would supervise twelve reporters. I would have a private office and the best part is that my salary would double. We could move to San Diego and you wouldn't have to work until you found a job you liked. "

"Sam that is absolutely wonderful. Did you accept the job?"

"I wanted to talk with you first. Do you still want to move to San Diego?"

"Yes, Sam. I do. I would love to be closer to your family for a couple of reasons. Sara would have an extended family and second so would I. When I think about my job, I can do what I do in any city of the United States."

Sam took me in his arms, "Jule I love you. How did you get me to marry you?"

"Who got who to marry who?" I teased Sam and we embraced and kissed. "Call the newspaper and accept the job. Get a start date and then we can strategize on when I will quit the firm. We also need to call your parents."

"Did you put all of that in writing?" Sam laughed as he punched in the newspaper's phone number. He talked with Susan from HR and they agreed upon a start date in a month. We had a lot to consider for the move. Sam called his parents and they were just as excited as we were. Sara said the cottage would be ready any day we wanted to arrive.

The next day, I talked with John, my boss, and gave him my resignation. "Julie, I can't tell you how sorry I am to see you leave.

You've become an exceptional lawyer. I will write a reference letter for you."

So that is the end of a five-year career and innumerable hours of research, late hours and court time preparation. In retrospect, what I have now in terms of a family, love and security goes far beyond my career.

We packed boxes, put in a change of address and went to goodbye lunches. Susan, from HR called to see what broker we were using to sell the house. "Andy from Houses for Sale," I read her the phone number and e-mail address from Andy's card.

"You do know that we will take over working with your agent in the sale of your home. All you have to do is pack, schedule a mover and send us the bill for reimbursement."

Three weeks later we were on the road to San Diego and the moving truck was right behind us. We arranged to have our furniture stored because the guest cottage was furnished and small, but very doable. Sara was approaching six months old and was developing quite a personality. She had Sam's blue eyes and blond surfer hair. When I watched her playing with her cousins, I knew we had made the right decision.

During the months following our move, I was so very happy. Sam loved his job and I didn't even look for a job. Sam's income was sufficient for our little family. I was a bit concerned that Sara and Corey would suffocate us with their attention, but they gave us our space. I spent time on the beach with Sara, learned to cook – really cook and I volunteered at a women's shelter providing legal advice to abused women.

# Chapter Nineteen

"We always take the same vacation every year. It is either to Hawaii or Mexico. Why don't we ditch the beaches and do a hike in the mountains."

"Because we don't know anything about hiking."

"Then we should do some research, hike the hills around here and get some experience."

We had the same conversation every year. I was a beach lover and Sam went with me because, well because he just went with me. However, this year he was insistent upon an inland excursion. It was January and time to plan our annual vacation.

"Jule, we are in such a good place. Mom, or one our sister-in-law's, will take care of little Sara and we can go off for a week or so by ourselves. Sara will be eight months old this summer and really won't miss us."

"Perhaps you're right, Sam. Have you thought about a place to go hiking?"

"Yes and no. We can either hike in the States, or go to another country, like Peru."

"Hmm, you've been doing some overseas stories. What do you think of an adventure in a jungle?"

"As you serious?"

"No, but it would be fun to go out of the country. I don't think we should do it alone. I'm sure there are guides that can take us on a trip, feed us and make sure we don't get lost."

A month passed and Sam didn't bring up a hiking trip. I assumed we would vacation in San Diego as we had the past year.

"Jule, remember the hiking excursion I suggested."

"Yes."

"Well, I have an idea. Let's not go out of the country for our first hike. How about we go on a short hike, just the two of us. We couldn't get lost if we went a short distance into the forest and we wouldn't be bogged down with a guide having to put up with people who are obnoxious or boring."

"And just where did you find us this romantic place?"

"Just hear me out. I've always heard about the Coronado National Forest in the southeast corner of Arizona and border of New Mexico. It is a national monument that is little known to most of the world."

Sam got out a map and we found the Coronado National Forest. "It seems a bit remote." I said.

"That's what we are looking for. We could go to Yosemite, but it is so crowded you'd hate it."

"Do you have any brochures on Coronado, or have you talked to anyone who has been there?"

"Sweetheart, I have brochures, maps, hiking trails and campsites."

"OK," I laughed. "I'm game. I do have a suggestion before we go off on an Indian Jones adventure."

"What is that?"

"Let's hike up in the Cuyamacas Mountains outside of San Diego. We might even consider a survival training class."

"I understand hiking but a survival class?"

"I don't even know how to start a campfire or set up camp, let alone how to look for someone who is lost. I just think we need to consider emergencies on a hiking trip."

"Honestly, Jule. I never even thought about that. Guess I've been in the city too long."

Little Sara started whimpering. It was late and I knew she was sleepy. "Sam, play Sara her lullaby. She loves to hear you sing and play."

"Will you sing with me?"

We made sure Sara was ready for bed and tucked under her Cinderella bed covers. Sam began to play and I was still as mesmerized by his melodious voice as I was the first night we met. I rocked Sara in her crib as Sam and I sang the lullaby he wrote for Sara.

*Sara, with her beautiful eyes of blue,*
*Sara, with her golden hair like dew.*
*Close your eyes in sleepy time,*
*And wait for angels' wings to chime.*
*Sara, with your eyes of blue,*
*Your Mommy and Daddy love you.*

The lullaby always lulled Sara to sleep by the last stanza. "Any chance I can work the same magic with you, only I want to lull you to bed and loving." Sam was looking at me with the same love he shared with Sara. "Sweetheart, now that Sara is asleep, that is entirely possible."

# Chapter Twenty

The next day while Sam was at work and Sara was down for her nap, I got out the brochures, maps and hiking information Sam brought home the evening before. I had no idea where the Coronado National Forest was. It really wasn't as remote as I thought last night and there were lots of hiking trails so we would run into people along the hike. The more I read about the area, the more excited I got. We had gotten used to vacationing on the beach and forgot there are other types of recreation. I also got out a map of southern California and looked up the Cuyamaca Hiking Trails.

When Sam got home, I told him I had reviewed the material extensively. Sam was happy that I was excited about the trip and we talked about what we would need to do get prepared over the next few months. By the end of the evening, we had an extensive list and now needed to put together an action plan with dates. We planned to check into a survival school, research hiking trails in the Cuyamacas, buy hiking boots, hiking and camping gear, and do a couple of overnight hiking trips. This is how we planned vacations. A seed got started in one of us and then our trip grew into a giant tree. We planned to go sometime in July, August or September. It depended upon when Sam could get the time off. I knew one of our sister-in-law's or Sara would take care of little Sara.

At Corey's suggestion we hired, Stan, a personal trainer to help us get in shape. We ran on the beach and took walks, but that was nothing compared to hiking at altitudes and rough terrain. Stan took us through a total body workout to strengthen our lower body and a program to strengthen our upper body to prepare us to hike with a thirty-pound backpack. Our last schedule was a progressive endurance program to get us in shape to climb elevations. At the end of four weeks, we were in the best shape either of us had ever been in.

It was now time for our survival course. When I researched classes, I found an organization in southern California that gave private courses. This was perfect and the course was only a day long. We learned about overnight camping, edible plants, how to track animal and human tracks, how to read a compass, starting a fire with and without a fire source, purifying natural water supplies, locating materials for covered sleeping and living quarters, the importance of having a means of protection like a gun, and what to do when faced with a wild animal. We left the class just after five o'clock and were more than a little overwhelmed.

"It's a good thing we didn't buy our camping gear and supplies because we would have bought the wrong things." Sam was looking at the sample purchase list of supplies as we left the building. "I think we should start with the basics and work our way up to what we want after we do a couple of overnight camping trips in the Cuyamaca Mountains."

Feeling fit and our basic overnight camping supplies purchased, we picked the second week in July for our first hike in the Cuyamaca Mountains. We drove the interstate from San Diego to a turn off to the Cuyamacas. It was amazing how we went from sea level and the beach to over 5,000 feet to a forest in such a short time. We stopped at a turnout in the road where we parked the Jeep, put on our backpacks and started up a trail that told us where we were and where we needed to be. The first part of the trail was new and exciting. We had made sure we had enough water to keep hydrated and rested every thirty minutes or so.

"Jule, keep quiet and turn very slowly to your left." I followed Sam's instructions and not far from us was a doe with a fawn. Seeing animals during the day was unusual. As soon as the mother saw us, she and her little one bolted. We hiked until noon and then found a cool spot by a stream to have lunch. After eating our power bars, dried fruit and fruit drink, we laid down and we both fell asleep for an hour.

"It's time we hit the trail. According to the trail map, we can camp in a spot about three hours away." Sam was pointing down the trail as he read. The hike for the most part was pleasant, however, the backpacks grew heavy by midafternoon and we took more rest breaks. "Sam, look there is a lake up ahead. Isn't this the lake for overnight camping on the brochure?"

"Yes, it is and I am ready to be somewhere," Sam said with a sigh.

The rest of the afternoon was occupied with setting up our two-person tent, preparing logs for a fire in the evening and setting out our camping foods. After we were assured we had our camp secured, we wandered out into the woods where there were no trails. Soon the forest got thicker and we found our hiking shorts didn't protect us against the twigs and low growing plants. "Sam, let's go back. I'm getting cuts, scratches and bites on my legs." Sam was only too happy to return.

Back at camp, I told Sam I wished he could have brought his guitar. "What is to prevent us from singing? We know most of our favorite songs by heart and there is no one around to hear us." Sam started out with a folk song and I soon picked up the melody. We were singing in harmony and provided a concert to any of the animals in the forest who cared to listen.

We had a scrumptious dinner of dried camping food when my legs began to itch. Thinking it was dry skin from the high altitude, I didn't say anything to Sam. It wasn't long before the itching turned into welts and then little vesicles. "Sam, take a look at my legs. They itch terribly and I'm miserable." Sam looked and suggested we call his father for advice on what the rash was and how to take care of it. He punched in his dad's number on his cell phone. There was no cell service. "Why didn't the survival course tell us about wilderness rashes?" Sam questioned while he looked for something in his backpack.

"What are you looking for?"

"Our survival book. Surely there is a chapter on rashes." Finding the book, Sam flipped through pages and then he stopped and read. "Jule, you have poison ivy. Have you ever had this before?" It confirmed that I had never been exposed to poison ivy in the past. "It shows a picture of a person with poison ivy and it looks just like your rash. Regardless of what the rash is from, it seems the best treatment in the wilderness is to keep the skin cooled with water. Let's go down to the lake and see if it works."

The cool water felt heavenly and we moved our camp closer to the water's edge. We had planned to camp two nights, but with my rash we headed home the next day. As soon as we got home, we looked for Sam's parents, both physicians, who could give me a diagnosis. We found Corey by the pool. He looked at my legs and said, "Poison ivy doesn't grow in this part of the country but poison oak does. The best treatment is cool compresses and calamine lotion." It took another ten days for the rash to disappear and an additional ten days for me to even consider a hiking excursion.

A few weeks later, we went on a hiking trip to a different part of the Cuyamacas. We both wore long pants and long-sleeved shirts. We also stayed on the trails and didn't venture into the woods. There were no mishaps and we found hiking was getting easier. Upon our return home, we felt ready to hike the Coronado National Forest and made plans to leave the first week of September.

# Chapter Twenty-One

"Do we have everything?" Sam asked.

"We have hiking shoes, clothes, tent, sleeping bags, food and water, survival book, first aid kit, medications, compass, survival pack, flashlights, extra batteries and camera."

"Then let's hit the road." We kissed little Sara and gave her extra hugs and handed her to Sam's mom. "Don't worry, we'll be okay while you're gone. Call when you can and have a wonderful trip." Sara and little Sara waved goodbye.

The drive was just under ten hours and we drove through mostly desert. Sam and I took turns driving and we sang a lot. "Too bad we couldn't bring your guitar," I said and Sam looked at me with a smile. "You brought your guitar," I said.

"I bought the smallest Ukulele they make and it is light enough that I am going to try and hike with it."

"And how about a romantic bottle of Napa wine?"

"I think I added that in at the last minute. Plastic bottles make a great carry vessel."

As we neared the Coronado National Forest, we saw fewer and fewer cars. We were driving from basically sea level to somewhere around 8,000 feet. This time we decided to drive the Jeep along the driving trails until we came to the Jack Rabbit campground and trail. We arrived late afternoon and had planned to have a relaxing evening and then backpack from the campground. When we arrived at the campground, we were surprised to find that it was nearly full. We drove around until we found tent camping. As we were setting up, there were several children running around screaming. "Do you think they belong to someone other than our neighbors?" I asked Sam. Just as he was about to respond, a rather large unkempt man came out of a large tent and screamed at the kids. "So much for hoping they belong elsewhere."

Reluctantly, we took our camping and hiking gear out of the Jeep as the children continued to scream and be unruly. Thirty minutes later, Sam went over to our camping neighbors and asked if they could settle their kids down. What occurred next happened quickly. The male neighbor told Sam to get the fuck away from his campground and proceeded to punch Sam in the face. Sam fell to the ground with blood running from his nose.

"You had no right to do that," I screamed and ran to Sam.

"Then get a lawyer," the fat man spat.

"I am a lawyer and I will press charges if you as much as come near our campground."

It didn't appear that Sam's nose was broken. "Julie, let's get out of here." We quickly packed the Jeep and took off. Approximately a mile down the road we realized we were not on the main driving road. "We'll be OK and when we find a place to pull off, we can set up camp there," Sam said in his most reassuring voice. We drove another two miles. The terrain became rockier and we didn't see a campground. "Is there anything on the map?"

"No, I think we are on land that isn't for hikers or campers." By this time, it was dusk and we knew we needed to find a place to camp for the night that was safe. Just as nighttime was falling, we spotted a piece of land nestled in the trees that was fairly level. We parked the Jeep, looked around the area and it seemed to be safe. The Jeep was unloaded in no time and our campsite set up.

"Sweetheart, if you will open that Napa Valley plastic wine container, I will fix a gourmet dinner out of our backpacks." Sam laughed and poured two glasses of wine in tin cups. "I wonder if this fancy restaurant has any music," I asked.

"My Dear, If you weesh, you shall have zee best music by zee best guitar player." I laughed and Sam played his new Ukulele which sounded wonderful in the forest. I hummed along and added water to our dried Beef Stroganoff.

Dinner was amazingly good with a glass of wine under the stars. We were both tired and by nine o'clock we were tucked into our sleeping bags in our two-person tent. The night sounds were lulling and we were asleep in minutes.

I was suddenly awake and heard a noise outside of our tent. I shook Sam and indicated he should be quiet. I whispered that I heard a noise and it was not an animal. It sounded more like someone going through our things. We hadn't locked the Jeep and we had left Sam's gun inside. We remained inside the tent and were still until we didn't hear anymore noises. Sam then ventured outside to look around. "Jule, come on out. You were right, there was someone here. Look at our campground. It's ransacked. The cooler is turned over and the fire wood scattered."

We walked to the Jeep together and found the unlocked doors had been opened and left open. We didn't think anything was taken. This was all too bizarre. Who would ransack a campsite and not take anything. We went back to our tent, talked for a while and then tried to get some sleep.

The next morning, we had breakfast and made an attempt to forget the incident. After all what could we do about it in the middle of nowhere? "Sam, where is our survival book?"

"Isn't it in the Jeep?"

"No, I looked and it's gone."

Sam said that it was bound to show up.

We decided to take a short hike. Since our campsite was not on the map, we didn't have any marked trails.

'll take the compass and we can mark our trail as we go," Sam reassured me.

"Sam, after last night I would feel more comfortable if you took your gun."

"I've already got it on my belt." We started off walking on what looked like a prior made trail. After an hour, I had the eerie feeling that someone was following us. Sam thought I was being too cautious, but I couldn't get rid of the feeling. At one point, I whispered to Sam to stop and not move. "There it is, hear the twigs snap?" Sam grinned and reminded me we were in the forest with animals and it was most likely a deer or other animal.

We sat down on a fallen log to rest. Sam laid our camera down and we wandered off to see the source of what sounded like falling water. What we found was an enormous water fall. "Sam, can you get a picture of the water fall?" Sam asked where the camera was and I told him he was carrying it.

"Jule, I don't have it. I laid it down on the log and thought you picked it up." We went back to where we thought we left the camera. To the contrary, the camera was gone.

"Sam, I don't like this. We are out in the middle of nowhere and no one knows where we are. Someone is following us."

"Jule, I don't know what to make of it and I'm not sure what we should do. Let's go back to camp and see if anything has been disturbed."

I listened all the way back to camp and didn't hear the same twig snapping sounds I heard on the way out. When we got back to camp, Sam told me to start looking through the camping gear and he would check the Jeep." Neither of us found anything out of place.

"Julie, we're miles from the main road and there is nothing we can do tonight. Let's get a good night's sleep and make some plans in the morning."

I brushed my teeth and got out my evening vitamins and birth control pills. The pills were not there. "Sam, my birth control pills are missing."

"Are you sure you brought them along?"

"Yes, I'm sure. This is getting too freaky."

"It's almost like someone is stalking us. We hear noises, but they can't be accounted for. We have things missing, but they're not high-priced items. Someone wants us to know they are here."

"Who could that be? We have no enemies or people who would wish us harm."

"I think we should stay awake tonight and see if we can catch whoever is doing this to us. Julie, I will take the first shift."

"Sweetheart, there is no way I will fall asleep with you on guard and some pervert in the woods. As of now, you have a co-guard."

And, so we sat and listened for anything unusual. Soon we were both asleep and then he/she came and slashed all four tires on the Jeep. When we woke up the sun was coming over the horizon. Thinking that we survived the night from our intruder, we yawned and greeted the sun thankful we were alive and together.

The most important thing to us was water. Yet, when we woke up our water supply was gone. "Sam, now what do we do? We can't survive without water."

"I know sweetheart. Here is the situation, we have no water and no way to get out of here with four slashed tires. We have no phone reception and our food will only last another two days. We need to walk down the way we came up."

"How many miles do you think we are from the main road?

"I figure we are about ten miles from that campsite with the rowdy kids. Let's take what we need and lock the rest in the Jeep."

"Should we take the sleeping bags and tent?"

"Yes, we'll probably need them." We were packed up in no time, the Jeep was locked and we started walking. At least Sam had his gun. When I asked how much ammunition he had he said told me he didn't pack any extra ammo. Sam took his gun out of his belt holster and popped out the clip. "There is no ammo in the clip and only one in the chamber."

"Then you had better be a good shot. Sam I just had a thought. Remember that water fall we found yesterday? We could back track and fill our water bottles up. We won't do well walking ten miles without water." And so, we turned around and left our campsite. After an hour of walking on yesterday's unmarked trail, I asked Sam, "Are you sure this is the right way?"

"No. Try listening for the water fall. Then we can follow the sound."

We walked another hour. "Sam, I think we are going the wrong way." Sam held up his hand, "Listen, do you hear that?" It was the sound of water falling. We climbed over rocks and boulders in the direction of the sound. "Wouldn't you think we could find the river the waterfall is making?" We continued making our way over the rocky terrain when I heard Sam yell.

"Julie, we found it. Excited, we jumped up and down and hugged each other. "Come on, we don't have far to go." In another thirty minutes, we were at the water's edge. "This is the reason we didn't find a river. The water is falling into a lake bed."

We decided to take a brief rest and split a protein bar. In order to get water, we had to walk a short distance to the water's edge. Sam wandered further around the lake and drank some of the cool water. I stayed and filled up our water vessels. We splashed in the water and acted like a couple of kids out on an adventure. When we got back to where we left our back packs, Sam's was gone.

"Sam, I can't do this anymore. There is someone stalking us and we're going to die out here." I started crying hysterically and Sam couldn't console me.

"Come on Julie, you're stronger than this. There is nothing we can do except buck it up and try to get back. I'll carry your backpack and you can follow me down the rocks."

Drying my tears, I followed Sam. We walked for a couple of hours and nothing looked familiar. "Sam, shouldn't we have come to our Jeep and campsite by now?"

"I would think so." Sam took out the compass from his pocket. "It says we are going due west and that's the direction we came from last night. Let's walk a little farther. A little farther got us further and further into the forest.

"I don't like this, Sam."

"I don't either."

"What should we do?"

"For now, keep walking."

I kept thinking about little Sara and what would she do without her parents. Her lullaby song sang in my head, over and over again. Soon I was humming her song. I hummed quietly so Sam wouldn't hear me, but he did. He stopped and turned around to face me and took me in his arms. "We'll get out of this mess. I promise you Julie."

I wept on his shoulder and when I looked up, I saw a small cabin peeking out from a grove of trees. "Sam, look! I see a cabin. Come on let's take a look." We walked as fast as we could through the thick forest. Sure enough, it was a cabin. We walked up to the door careful not to fall over or through the rotting boards. No one answered our knocks on the door. We carefully opened the door and saw that someone was living there. "Let's wait on the front porch for the owner to come home." Sam followed me out to the front porch. We shared another protein bar and drank from our water vessel. We passed the next couple of hours talking about little Sara, how we met and our move to San Diego. "Do you miss not practicing law?" Sam asked.

"Yes and no. I miss the drama of the courts, but not the heart-breaking stories and lives of my clients. I have also found that being a mom and wife is the most fulfilling job I could have."

"Should we make more babies?"

"I was thinking along those lines."

"Hey! What 'er doin on my property?" A gruff voice came out of nowhere and we jumped off of the porch.

"Ah, we were waiting for you to come back. You see we are

a little lost and are trying to find our way back to our campsite."

"Y'er a bunch of greenhorns is what you are. I ain't seen no one this far in the forest for a long time. What's a couple of kids like you doin up here"

"Sir, if you could help us get back down the mountain, we would be most appreciative." I said in my most calm voice.

"Where's y'er camp'in gear?"

"It's all a long story," Sam began.

"Well, come on in. Ain't no use stand'n out here when we can sit in chairs."

"Thank you mister, ah?"

"Ain't no mister. Name's Harry, Harry Spit. Folks 'round here call me Harry the Spit," Harry said with a guffaw laugh.

"Well, Harry could we plug in our cell phone to charge it?" Sam asked as he pulled out his cell phone.

"Ain't got no 'lectricity and ain't got no telee phone."

Sam and I looked at each other in despair. We had no way to call for help.

Harry sat down at a roughly made table. "So, tell me kids, how ye' come to get to these parts?"

Sam told Harry about our hiking and camping vacation. He then went over the details of our stalker and how our things kept disappearing.

"That feller has been stalkin' folks for the past year. Ain't nobody seen him, but he usually comes in the night. Takes the gall durndest things. One time he took a little kid's stuffed bear.

"Has he ever hurt anybody?"

"Not yet, but he sure as the devil puts a hell of a scare into folks."

"Harry, we would like to find our way down the mountain. Can you help us?"

"Well kids, it's this a'way. I ain't got no horse and that is the only way you 'all is go'in to get down this here mountain 'ceptin to walk. My guess is that your folks will be worried about you 'all and send out a search party when you 'all don't come home."

"Of course," Sam remembered. "In survival school they said that if you are lost the best thing to do is to stay put and wait for help to arrive."

"You'all is welcome to stay a couple days. Ain't had no company for near a year now."

"Harry, we don't know how to thank you," Sam offered his hand to Harry in a handshake. Harry ignored Sam's hand and got off his wooden stool and stood up.

"Ain't got but one room, so you'd be better off sleep'n outside." Harry didn't wait for an acceptance of his offer. "Now geet along so's in I can geet someth'n done."

What Harry had to "geet done" was unknown because he was out on the porch smoking his pipe.

We set up our tent and had no change of clothes or toiletries. The afternoon was spent talking with Harry who seemed hungry for conversation. "How did you come to live in the forest and this house?"

"I was a state trooper and got tired of see'n folks geet killed and kids on drugs. One day 'bout ten years ago, I up and started walk'n through the forest. I knew'd I wasn't com'n home so when I saw'd this here cabin, I homesteaded it." Sam and I laughed.

"What about your family?"

Harry was quiet for a moment. "My wife and son were kill't in a car accident. Got hit by a drunk driver." There was nothing to say, so Sam and I were quiet.

"Say, I exp't you kids are a mighty bit hungry. Care to share my grub with me tonight?"

"Harry, we'd love to. What can we do to help?" Sam and I stood up and followed Harry into the cabin.

"You can geet some farwood out behind the cabin. Don't like to heat the cabin up 'les it is cold outside."

Sam collected the firewood and Harry soon came out and started a fire in his rock fire ring. He had a metal rod that he hung a large pot on. As the food got warm, it smelled delicious.

"Harry, what are you cooking?" I asked.

"Darl'n best you not know."

We had the best stew either of us had ever eaten and we didn't ask Harry what was in it. We learned that Harry lived off of the land finding eatable plants and he killed only what he needed for food. I could see the cogs in Sam's brain starting to go around. This would be a great human interest story for the newspaper. Harry didn't have any writing paper or pencils. Sam would have to rely on his memory for notes.

That night lying in our tent, I asked Sam how long he thought it would take for his parents to realize we were missing. "I've been thinking about that. I told mom and dad that we would be home a week from the day we left. We have now been gone four days, so at the earliest they would worry in another couple of days. Especially when we don't call and they can't get ahold of us."

We spent the next few days exploring the forest, but not venturing very far. One day, when we returned, we found Harry was not home. We also found our tent had been torn down. "Oh my gosh, the stalker has found us." I told Sam we needed to warn Harry when he returned.

"Darl'n that old fella is only look'n for someth'n to do. He ain't hurt nobody yet." Harry told us when he got back to the cabin.

"Have you ever seen him?" Sam was interviewing Harry without him knowing it was happening.

"Nope." That was the end of the interview.

It had been a week since we left our last campsite and walked to find water. Sam began to complain of abdominal cramps and diarrhea.

"Honey, I think you picked up a bug somewhere." After the first day, Sam could no longer function and spent the day in our tent and running into the forest to 'crap' as he called it. Harry took notice of Sam's behavior. "What part of the lake did you 'all drink from?"

he asked me as we watched Sam run into the woods.

"It was on the south side. The water was calm and looked clear." I looked at Harry wondering why he was asking me about where we got our water.

"Ther's a bug from that ther part of the lake that causes a sickness like y'er fella has now."

I went back in my mind to our survival training. Of course, I thought. There is a bacteria called gia . . . something that causes abdominal cramping and diarrhea. As I recall, it causes dehydration.

Sam couldn't keep any liquids down and food became a word unspoken around him. He had a fever and was becoming a bit delirious. On the fourth day, I saw a hiker coming towards the cabin. I ran to him, "Oh my gosh. You don't know how happy I am to see you."

"And you have no idea how hard it has been to track you down." It was then that I saw his shirt said Arizona Search and Rescue Team. "Your folks contacted the Forest Ranger Station when you didn't let them know you were off the mountain and they couldn't contact you. Let me guess, you had no phone reception and your phone was dead."

"How did you know?"

"Happens too many times. Now, where's your husband?"

"He's in the tent and is very sick. He probably needs to be in a hospital." We walked to the tent and found Sam moaning and holding his abdomen. "Harry, the man who lives here, thinks he drank some contaminated water." The rescue worker was on his walkie talkie and calling for a helicopter.

"The chopper will be here in thirty minutes. Gather up what you want to take back with you." Harry walked over to the rescue worker, "Hi 'ya Steve. How's it goin?"

How did these two men know each other? Steve turned to me, "Harry and I go back a long way. We were state troopers together." Steve and Harry were catching up on whatever they found interesting to talk about. I had gathered up the few belongs we had and noticed that Sam had a liquid stool in his sleeping bag. I fetched some water and cleaned him up the best I could. Just as I finished, I heard the helicopter landing. It only took minutes to load Sam in to the chopper and I had only a few seconds to give Harry a hug and thank him. "Jest don't tell no body where I live."

Steve and I boarded the chopper with Sam and we were on our way to the hospital in Tucson. As soon as we landed, I called Sara and Corey and let them know we were now safe. They made arrangements with their physician sons to cover their practice and drove the six hours to Tucson. I tried to get them to stay home, but they refused telling me we would need a car to get back to San Diego and they were right.

With several liters of intravenous fluids, Sam was less listless and knew me. "Where am I?" I filled him in on the past couple of days. "Do you remember Harry?"

"You betcha and I have the story in my head." We both laughed.

"Sam, the last thing Harry told me when the chopper was taking off was not to tell anyone where he lived."

"Well, sweetheart, there are always fictitious locations and cabins."

Three days later, Sara and Corey drove us home. They had taken charge of the situation which was fine with us. I was in need of being taken care of, just as Sam was, and we missed little Sara terribly.

A Year Later

"Sweetheart, here is your human interest story about Harry on the front page of the San Diego paper." We had decided to wait a year to print the story to protect Harry's privacy. It was a wonderful story and our privacy was also protected.

When we returned from Arizona, we talked about our new hiking and camping careers and decided to return to the beaches for our vacations. After all, we had had enough with a stalker, having our belongings ransacked and stolen, getting lost in the woods, ingesting contaminated water, Sam coming down with Giardia, losing cell phone service and finding Harry and his cabin.

"Who is sending you flowers?" Sam asked seeing the large bouquet on the table.

"Well now, take a look at the middle of the flowers." I said with a grin.

"Julie, you're pregnant?" Sam asked with an enormous smile when he found the blue booties in the middle of the flower arrangement.

"Yes, and you missed something. Look further."

"There are a pair of pink booties."

"Yep."

"We are going to have twins?"

"Yep."

"Julie, I love you." Sam picked me up from the sofa and swung me around the room.

"I know."

I always knew why I met Sam on vacation when he lived in San Francisco and I lived in Sacramento. We met in San Francisco and fell in love.

# Seven Kittens

# Introduction

Have you ever seen a litter of new kittens? Then you know this is one of the miracles of nature. Whether they are several days, or several weeks old these adorable little sacks of fur are soft looking with tiny paws and big eyes. Like all newborn animals, including humans, kittens are innocent and rely solely upon their mother for nourishment, nurturing and protection. Without their mom, they will die. This is the story of seven-liter mates who found love and devotion with their human families.

# Chapter One

"Hey, Sis. Where are you?"

"I don't know. This is different than where we were before."

"There were more of us and it was dark."

"Well, Sis. It's still dark, but we aren't in our nice warm bath any longer."

"Wait, I think someone bumped into me. Why can't we see?"

"Let's all bundle up together and try to stay warm."

"I'm hungry."

"So am I."

"Now who is that?"

"Sounds like a guy. How many do you think there are of us?"

"I am going to nose around and see if I can get a count."

"Wouldn't there be the same number we had when we were in our warm bath?"

"How would I know," the gruff kitten voice said.

"Oops, that makes five of us. Hey, who else is with us?"

"Me and me."

"Well, then. There are seven of us, five girls and two boys."

"Don't we have a mom?"

"Sure, we have a mom, everybody has a mom."

"Mom, where are you?" One of the little girl kittens meowed.

Suddenly, there was a big movement and we were all tossed about.

"I smell milk." Now all I have to do is find the milk before everyone else does. Gruff kitty was on the prowl for milk.

"Not so fast, buster," a little girl kitten said. "I think we can all share in the milk. After all, it seems there are enough spigots."

Just then we heard the sweetest mom voice say, "Children, there is enough for everyone. Just line up and I'll lie down for you."

And that's just what we did. We couldn't see, but we could certainly smell. Mom's milk was the best and we all took a nap after we ate.

It seems we slept and ate a lot in the beginning. We stayed warm when mom was with us, but when she went out, we got cold and lonely. We didn't know where she went, we just knew we missed her and our meows didn't always bring her back right away. So, we stayed together because there was danger on the outside.

One day a few of us started to open our eyes. Our eyesight wasn't great yet but we could tell we were all different. Some of us looked like little tigers with stripes. Others were one color and our fur was different lengths. We also couldn't hear very well, so we were content to stay in our little warm bed with mom.

In the beginning, we didn't move around much because, well, we just couldn't. When we were about four weeks old, our little wobbly legs were stronger and we found we could explore our home. If we tried to go any further, mom would grab us by the scruff of the neck and bring us back to our litter of brothers and sisters. We figured mom knew best, but we sure wanted to see what was outside of our small world. We found out that once our eyes were opened, we needed to explore and move about and climb and poke around into anything that we could get into.

# Chapter Two

When we were about five weeks old, mom went out and never came back.

"Where's mom?" we all asked. Soon we were all meowing loudly because we were hungry, frightened and lonely."

"We can't survive without mom. How are we going to get milk?"

We didn't know what to do other than meow for mom. We also knew better than to try and leave the safety of our home.

It wasn't too much later that we heard a strange voice. It wasn't another kitten, but it was young, sweet and kind.

"Mom, look here are the kittens. They're so cute. We need to take them home and try to feed them."

"Molly, go into the house and get a shoe box from my closet and line it with a towel. I'll wait here for you."

The second human voice was older but was also kind and caring. Why would Molly need a shoebox?

Suddenly, the second human voice had a hand that picked up one of our sisters. "Shhh, little one. Your mama was killed by a car and we are going to take care of you." She put our sister down and we all cuddled together tighter.

"I got the biggest shoe box I could find and the softest blanket. Can I pick them up?"

"Yes, but be careful. They are pretty little and have sharp claws."

"It must be terrible to live in a junk yard and be born under an old shed."

"You are right, darling. But they were safe here with their mom until they got old enough to start venturing out on their own."

"What are they talking about?" Gruff Kitty asked.

"I don't know. It isn't kitty talk but it sounds nice. I wonder where we're going. This is a new kind of house and it's moving. I'm going to try to crawl out of here."

"Oh, no you don't," the older human voice said as she put our brother back in the box.

"Hey, I am going to try to climb out," a sister said as she started climbing out of the box and almost made it."

"Mom, that one is getting out," the youngest human voice yelled.

That word, 'mom', got our attention. We knew that word and it meant that our mom was coming home to take care of us. How was she going to get into this moving box? All at once, we began meowing thinking it would bring mom home to us.

"They must be hungry. "How do we feed them?" the younger voice asked?

"Let's call Roscoe's vet. She'll know how to feed kittens."

The two human voices set us down and put some sort of top on the box. We could see through the top, but we couldn't get out of our moving vessel.

# Chapter Three

"Dr. Westin," this is Roscoe's mom. "We just found a litter of kittens. Their mom was killed by a car in front of our house and we found the kittens under an old shed in the abandoned lot next door. They are adorable and they need to be fed, which is why I am calling."

"How many kittens are in the litter and how old do they appear to be?"

"There are seven kittens and I don't know exactly how old they are. Their eyes are open, and their gait is a little wobbly."

"Hmm, sounds like they are probably a month or so old. It's too bad they couldn't be with their mom for another two months. Nevertheless, you called me about feeding the kittens.

They need mother's milk and we have a cat formula you can purchase to feed them. We also have kitten bottles and nipples."

"How often do they need to be fed?"

"They should be on a feeding schedule every three hours and that includes during the night."

"Oh my, I'm not sure I can do that with work and Molly has school. Is there any place we can take them?"

"There's a cat rescue place just outside of town called the Kit Kat House. I don't know if they are taking any new kittens, but it's certainly worth a try."

"What about the humane society?"

"They do take kittens, but if they aren't adopted out, they

are euthanized."

"Oh, dear. I can't let that happened. Thank you, Dr. Westin."

The nice, kind lady's voice stopped talking and came over to look at us. "You poor kitties. We need to find someone who can look after you."

"Mom, what did the vet say?"

"Molly, the kitties need to be fed every three hours and we can't take on that responsibility right now."

"Then what are we going to do? They need to eat."

"Dr. Westin told me about a place that takes in kittens. I'm going to give them a call. I'm sure the little kitties are hungry by now."

"We have to let this new person know that we are hungry," one of the little sister kittens meowed. "Let's all meow at the same time."

And so all seven kittens started meowing at the same time.

"Mommy, they're hungry," the young human voice said.

"I know darling. I just found the phone number of the Kit Kat House and I'm going to call them."

It seemed like a long time before the nice lady was able to talk to someone on the phone. Then we heard her talking, but we couldn't hear anyone talking back.

"Hello, we found seven kittens under an abandoned shed this morning. Their mother was killed by a car about an hour before we found them. I talked with our vet and she told me that you take in kittens and I wondered if you had room for these little darlings."

The nice lady was quiet and then she said, "You can take them, how wonderful. Yes, we can be there in an hour."

"Molly, they can take the kittens at the Kit Kat House. If you'll get the kittens, we can take them in now."

"Mom, they're so cute. Can't we keep at least one?"

"Sweetheart, they're too young and we don't know anything about taking care of kittens."

"Do you think we could adopt one after they get bigger?"

"Perhaps, now get the kittens."

Our new home started moving again. "Hey, where are we going now?" Gruff kitty meowed. "I'm going to get out of here."

"Me too," another kitty meowed.

"Mom, the kitties are trying to get out of their box."

"They must be frightened. Put a towel over the top of the box so they can't see what is happening."

"Whoa, why is it so dark in here?" Gruff Kitty asked. "We're moving again."

"Mom, mom, mom." All seven kitties started meowing for their mother not knowing they would never see their mother again.

"This is not good," the little black and white stripped kitty said. "Our house is moving, but it's different."

"I wonder if they asked our mom if it was OK to move us. Mom always got upset when we tried to leave our home," the little tuxedo girl kitty meowed.

It didn't seem to make a difference if the little kitties meowed, or not. So, one by one, the kittens became quiet.

"I wonder why our new house stopped moving." The white kitten with the black tipped tail asked.

"There are a lot of voices talking and it's not kitty talk. I wonder where we are." The twin to the white kitten with the black tipped tail said.

We could see the faces of the two human people who found us. They were looking at us and the littlest voice was crying. "Bye kitties," she said and then they were gone.

"Now what's going to happen to us?

"I don't know, but they'd better feed us," Gruff Kitty meowed.

# Chapter Four

"Aren't they adorable?" The human voices said. Now there were four human faces looking at us. "Let's see if Sassy will accept them. Her last litter of kittens has been weaned and she is still producing milk."

The kittens were put in a large container that had holes in the sides. "I don't think we can get through these holes," one of the sisters said.

"Yeah, but we can meow and maybe they'll let us out."

"Meowing will get you nowhere, little ones," a new human voice said. "Try letting Sassy and the kittens smell each other through the crate."

"This kitty smells like our mom. Come on everyone, our mom has come back."

"The kittens are coming to the side of the crate. They are either curious about Sassy, or they can smell her milk."

"Look they are trying to nuzzle Sassy through the crate. Let's see what happens when we put Sassy inside."

Sassy started purring in kitty talk to let the kittens know she was friendly and was going to feed them.

"I smell milk," Gruff Kitty meowed. "Get out of my way everyone, I am going to eat."

Sassy's purring changed its tone and Gruff Kitty wobbled back a few steps. "My darlings. I am your new mother and I have plenty of milk for everyone, including you," she looked at Gruff Kitty. "Let's see, there are seven of you and I have eight nipples, so everyone will have a place to nurse."

Sassy began to lick our fur and it felt just like our first mom's licking. When she got finished licking us one by one, we got a nipple and a place to eat.

"They are certainly hungry and it is good that Sassy has accepted the kittens. Of course, the kittens will need to be in isolation for a couple of weeks until we know they don't have any infections they could pass on to the other cats." We didn't understand this human talk, but at least we were together and had been fed. And, we got a new mom.

We were put in a large crate with Sassy. We spent most of our time sleeping and eating and we began to grow. We had the best time chasing each other around when the human people let us out of our crate. Sometimes it seemed like we were fighting, but we weren't and always snuggled with each other when it was nap time. Kitties can't tell time and we never knew what day it was. We just knew we were getting older and had a fierce need to explore our surroundings.

"Maude, I am worried about the kittens. They have these circular sores and some of the kittens are losing their fur."

"Kelly, we have a new young vet intern. Let's find out what she has to say."

Just then, a young woman in her mid-twenties came into the room. "Good morning, ladies," she said as she poured a cup of coffee for herself. "How are our star kittens doing?"

"Dr. Jeremy, we are so glad to see you. Kelly and I were talking that it is time to put the litter up for adoption. However, Kelly told me some of the kittens have circular sores and are losing their fur. Would you take a look at them?"

"Of course. Bring them to me one by one. As a precaution, please wear gloves and wash your hands between handling each kitten."

Kelly picked up Gruff Kitty who they named Growly Bear because he always growled at the staff and his siblings. "Maude and Kelly, you were observant to see these sores because they are just beginning. Growly Bear has ringworm and needs to be isolated. Please bring me another kitten."

Over the course of the next hour, all seven kittens were examined by Dr. Jeremy and placed in isolation. All of the kittens were infected and needed to be treated. Their lesions were in the typical places of the head, ears and forelimbs.

"Why is everyone looking at our skin and fur and muttering non-kitty talk?" One of the gray kittens asked. Her name was Jackie.

"Well, I certainly itch and am tired of scratching," another female meowed, named Peppermint.

"Oops, we are moving out of our home. Hey," we started meowing, "where are we going?"

No one would talk to us. In fact, they stayed away as if we had something wrong. Then we were placed in another crate and Sassy was with us. She wasn't sick, but she was treated as if she was sick. The humans left us alone and we did the only thing we knew how to do. We meowed and meowed and meowed. A lot of good it did us because no one came back.

Isabell, the yellow and white long-haired kitty, asked what we were going to do.

"Well, that is obvious," Snowflake said, the little white kitty with the black tipped tail.

"And, just what would that be?" her twin sister, Cotton Ball, asked.

"We must escape from this crate and run away." Snowflake meowed looking at her siblings.

"Okay, but you go first," Cotton Ball said to her twin.

"Just how are you going to pull this off?" Jake, our brother, asked Snowflake with a kitty sneer.

"I figure the humans are going to come back soon. They will want to open the crate to see how we are doing. Cotton Ball and I will make a break for it when the door is opened. They will be surprised because we haven't tried this before. The rest of you will distract the humans so we have a chance to get outside."

"What about the rest of us?" Isabell asked.

"You will be with Jake, Growly Bear, Jackie and Peppermint. We are old enough now and can run like the wind, so we should be able to get away with no trouble. Are you all with me?"

Everyone gave their meow of approval and waited. We didn't have to wait long until the humans came into the room.

"Kitties, we have a treat for all of you." Maude announced. "First we are going to rub a little cream on your skin and then we have some good tasting medicine."

"Peppermint, you can be first," Kelly said. Peppermint became frightened and tried to bite and scratch Kelly. The cream was okay, but the liquid medicine was bitter and made her foam at the mouth.

"Oh, dear, they are not going to like the oral medication," Maude said.

"Well, we have to do the best we can because they need this medication or they will never get rid of their ringworm and be adopted out."

The human voices tried to give all of us the medication and we all fought the process.

"Come on Cotton Ball, this is our chance." Snowflake was flicking her ears at Cotton Ball, the que to make a run for it. They scooted around to the corner of the crate that was open and ran out of the door.

"Maude, get those two kittens," Kelly yelled.

"Snowflake, I am scared." Cotton Ball meowed. There was such a commotion with the two white kitties running around the room. Suddenly, the big door opened and Snowflake ran out into the open yard. A strange furry animal was looking at her. Oh, my. What am I going to do? She had never seen a dog before and didn't know what a bark was. The dog barked and barked and Snowflake was frozen. One of the humans came out to the yard and tried to get the dog away. Suddenly, the human grabbed Snowflake by the scruff of her neck. The dog lunged at the human and Snowflake. The human was now scared and lessened her hold on Snowflake. Seeing her chance to get away, Snowflake turned her head and bit the human. The human dropped Snowflake and she ran up a tree. The dog continued to bark and Snowflake climbed higher and higher in the tree.

"Trixie, come back here." The dog's human owner came running into the yard and took hold of the dog by its lease. "I am so sorry," the owner said as she walked Trixie out of the yard.

Great. I'm now stuck up a tree. Maybe it wasn't so bad being in the crate with my sisters and brothers. What is going on down on the ground? A little human is climbing up the tree and calling my name. I didn't know humans could climb trees.

"Snowflake, come on Snowflake." The little human kept calling Snowflake's name and now he was very close to her. "You're OK, come on." Suddenly he picked her up by the scruff of the neck and climbed down the tree. So much for trying to escape.

A few days later, we heard the human voices talking about us. They seemed to think we needed to go to a foster home, whatever that was. "A foster mom has fewer kittens to look after and these kitties will get more attention with one mom," one of the humans said. And so, another chapter of our life was about to begin.

# Chapter Five

Rita was the director of the Kit Kat House and she was consulted about the seven kittens and the need for a foster mother. "I would suggest you call Ricky. She has been taking care of kitties for years," Rita told the human voices.

We heard someone on the phone calling Ricky and it sounded like she was coming to see us. "Let's get groomed so Ricky will want to take all of us," Jackie chimed in. She and Peppermint, rarely had anything to say. You do know that cats groom each other, and themselves several hours a day. So, this grooming session was not unusual. They finished grooming each other just as Ricky came to see them.

"Oh, my!" she replied. "They are darling kittens. Did you say that they need special attention to get them to take their medications?"

The human voices told Ricky about our medication rejection. That didn't seem to bother her. She told the human voices that she had no foster kittens at the moment and would love to take all of us.

Off we went in another moving box. This time we were bigger and we could see. We didn't like being moved. Tough Growly Bear and Jake threw up and two of the sisters had diarrhea. What a mess they made in the moving box. This didn't seem to bother Ricky. She just smiled and told us we would be home soon.

Ricky cleaned up all of us because we had poop and vomit on our fur from our siblings. She put us in a clean box. "Is this where we are going to live?" Snowball asked. "This is so small and we are getting big, how are we going to move around?"

Without too much time to think about our dilemma, we were transported into a large room. Ricky closed the door to the room and then opened up the box she used to transport us. "Okay, kitties. This is your new home. Come on out and see what you have to play with." Snowflake and Cotton Ball came out first, followed by Isabell and Peppermint. They were overwhelmed by the new room. "Come on everyone, this is wonderful," Isabell meowed. That prompted Growly Bear, Jake and Jackie to slowly come out of the box. There were kitty toys to climb in, around, over and under. In the corner of the room was a basket full of soft squishy toys. Ricky showed us what was called a cat tree that we could climb up and hide in.

This was so wonderful for the orphaned kittens and they soon forgot their original home under the old shed. They still thought about their mom and wondered why she never came home. But since the humans didn't understand kitty talk, they would never find out.

Ricky was a darling. We meowed when we were hungry and we meowed just to meow. Ricky put us on kitten food and we no longer needed our second mom, Sassy, for kitten milk. Sassy was sent back to the Kit Kat House to be a mom to other kittens.

Ricky spent time with us playing, petting and keeping us and the room clean. The petting and holding had something to do with becoming friendly with humans. She would coax us into taking our medications by using a special small syringe that she filled with the medicine and expertly squirted down our throats. There was no more throwing up or frothing at the mouth.

Because we were contagious, we had to stay in the one room for a very long time. Ricky would take a few of us at a time to the vet for checkups. We couldn't be put up for adoption until we were ringworm free.

# Chapter Six

It was a nice sunny day when Ricky came in with the cat carrier. We assumed we might be going outside or for a ride. We were used to going to the vet and this was another possibility. She picked up the five girls and put them in the carrier. "Hey, what about us?" Growly Bear meowed. Jake tried to crawl into the carrier. "Whoa, fella. Not so fast. You will get your turn soon." Ricky said as she picked up the carrier.

The girls began to meow and the boys soon joined in the chorus. "I'll be back soon," Ricky told Growly Bear and Jake.

"Now where do you suppose we are going?" Isabell asked. "I don't know, but Growly Bear and Jake should be going with us," Snowflake answered.

"Girls, we are going to the vet because it is time for you to be spayed. I know this makes no sense to you, but you'll be home tomorrow."

At the vet's office, Ricky greeted the front girl office, did some paperwork and then left us with an attendant. "I'll see you tomorrow," Ricky said as she petted each of us and then left.

"What is a spay?" Cotton Ball asked? "I don't know," Jackie answered. The kittens were afraid and instead of meowing, they were very quiet and huddled together in the corner of the carrier. Soon a nice young human girl came in and took the kittens out of the carrier and carried them to another room. They were put to sleep and didn't know what happened while they were sleeping.

"My tummy hurts," the kittens began to meow as they woke up. "What's this on our tummy and why don't we have any fur on our tummies?" Peppermint meowed. Just then the nice young girl came in and gave them all some medicine and they began to feel better. They slept most of the day and night until Ricky came to pick them up late the next morning to take them home.

"I'm sorry that you had to go through your surgery," Ricky talked to them on the way home. "You are old enough to get pregnant and we can't have kittens having kittens. Growly Bear and Jake are going in next week and they'll also be neutered."

The girl kittens recovered well and had their stitches out ten days later. Growly Bear and Jake were neutered and also recovered without any problems.

# Chapter Seven

"How old are we now?" Quiet Isabell asked.

"Let's see." Jake meowed. We were five weeks old when the nice human ladies took us from under the shed and then took us to another home."

"Then they found something wrong with us and put us in isolation," Snowflake added, "And Cotton Ball and I tried to escape."

"I think we were about seven weeks old when Ricky became our foster mom and Sassy went back to the home to be adopted," Jackie meowed.

"We have been with Ricky for a month." Growly Bear was asserting his male hood. "So, we have about two more weeks here with Ricky which would make us three months old and old enough to be adopted."

"Oh, my." Isabell meowed. "I simply don't want to leave everyone and all of our wonderful play toys."

"Isabell," Peppermint meowed quietly, "I don't see how we have much of a choice. We have to trust that Ricky will put us in good homes. Maybe some of us will go together."

# Chapter Eight

We all had appointments to see the vet the following week and were declared free from ringworm. That meant that we were approved for adoption.

Ricky got us all ready for the adoption center. She put bows in the girl's fur by their ears and the boys got little bowties. I will admit we looked darling.

Ricky took us in three carriers and we meowed most of the way to the adoption center. Didn't she know that cats hate to travel? And, with our last experiences traveling in a car, it meant a new home. When we got to the adoption center, we noticed that there were a lot of kittens and young cats in cages. There were notes on the front of the cage indicating the type of cat, how old they were and if they liked children, being petted, or other things a new owner should know.

Snowflake and Cotton Ball got adopted the first day to twin girls. It was their fourth birthday and their parents told them they could each pick out a kitten. We all meowed as they left and Snowflake and Cotton Ball watched us from their new cat carrier as they left the adoption center. That left five of us when we went home later that day.

We repeated the adoption process the following weekend and Growly Bear and Jake were adopted by a nice-looking elderly couple. They were looking for company and cats that liked to be petted. Now, one would think that Growly Bear wouldn't be affectionate. However, he would be the first one in a lap before any other kitties had a chance to hop up. Jake was our purring brother and he loved to be petted no matter where he was.

Now there were three of our original litter left, Jackie, Peppermint and Isabell, all little girls. We stayed with Ricky another two weeks before she took us to the adoption center. We missed our siblings. Ricky seemed to sense this and spent extra time with us. One evening she let us out of our room to explore her house. We had never seen anything so big. Isabell decided to scratch on the sofa and Ricky came over and picked her up and said, in a loud and authoritative voice, "no." Isabell knew immediately that she would not try to scratch on the sofa again. Ricky sat down to read while we explored and soon Isabell was in her lap. You could see contentment on Ricky's face as Isabell curled up and purred.

"Jackie, I think Isabell may have a new home." Jackie agreed and we gave each other a kitty paw high-five.

Isabell didn't go to the adoption center again. It was just Jackie and Peppermint that needed a new home.

Soon after being on display at the adoption center, a lady came in and told Ricky that she wanted to adopt a cat. "We have two cats left out of this litter for adoption. Their mother had seven kittens and she was killed by a car shortly after they were born."

"Oh, my goodness, they are cute. May I hold one of them?" The nice lady was given Jackie and she purred excessively. "May I see the other kitten?" Peppermint followed Jackie's suit and purred as loud as she could.

"This is perfect because I wanted two kittens."

"Really, you want two kittens?" Ricky asked in surprise.

"Yes, and I want them from the same litter and I want females."

Ricky was ecstatic because Jackie and Peppermint fit her request explicitly.

"Hey Jackie, I think we are going to a new home with this

nice lady."

"I think you are correct, Peppermint. Let's get ready for another car ride."

Then the nice lady left and the kitties were afraid she wouldn't come back, just like their first mom. "Okay, you little darlings. That nice lady just adopted you and went to buy some food, toys and supplies." Ricky said smiling.

We learned that the nice lady's name was Alex and when she returned, she had a carrier, litter box, litter, food, toys, combs and brushes. Her shopping cart was over flowing. We were put in the new carrier and meowed goodbye to Ricky as we were carried from the adoption center.

# Chapter Nine

Life was just about to get better. Alex sang all the way to our new home and we found that we didn't want to meow in protest about the car ride. "You are such good kitties," she said as she put her hand inside of our carrier to pet us while she was driving.

"Alex has a very nice voice and I love that she is petting us while we are in the car." Jackie purred to Peppermint.

Once we got to Alex's house, she put us in a room. "Oh no, are we going to have to live in one room?" Peppermint exclaimed with her meows.

"Girls, I have been told that you should spend the first twenty-four hours in one room to get used to your new home and then I can take you to a new room. I'll be right back with your food and water."

Alex left us and closed the door behind her. We were alone again without our siblings. We started doing what kitties do best. Yep, we started to meow and not just little meows, but those meows a human can't ignore.

It didn't take long before Alex came back into the room. "You know I'm going to break all of the kitty adoption rules and let you have the run of the house. Please, just don't hide behind the washer and dryer or refrigerator."

We had no idea what Alex said. We only knew that the door was open and we could explore. There were places where we could climb, jump and hide. Alex let us run around as she watched over us. After a while, we became very tired. Alex was sitting in her favorite chair and we both jumped into her lap and went to sleep.

"You two are so sweet. I will tell you that I'm not fond of your names and would like to rename you." Her voice woke us up and we looked up at her. "What did she say?" Peppermint purred. "I have no idea, but we should pay attention."

"Little Jackie, you remind me so much of my first kitty, Tigger, and I would like to name you after her. And Peppermint, I am going to name you after a little dog I had. Her name was Tassie. If it's OK with you both, you now have new names. "We should meow," the new Tigger said and so we meowed.

As sisters, Tigger and Tassie were the best of friends. They played together, slept together, groomed each other and even had kitty fights that really were not fights. Alex loved her new kittens, especially when they snuggled up tight with her in bed at night. You see, Alex had lost her husband and she was terribly lonely. For some reason, she felt her kitties knew about her loss.

One day about three months after Alex adopted Tigger and Tassie she went on a vacation and planned to be away for ten days or so. Two of Alex's friends came over to feed and look in on the kittens.

"Tigger," Tassie meowed. "Mom has gone away and hasn't come home yet. This is just like when our first mom went away and never returned. What are we going to do?"

"I don't know. There are two nice human ladies that come to feed us, but we don't have anyone to sleep with at night and keep us company all day long."

The two kittens were so stressed out that they started having bloody diarrhea and they threw up blood. Their stomachs hurt but they had no one to meow at in distress. This went on for several days and they wanted to go back to Ricky's house but had no way of leaving or getting to Ricky's. Then one day when they were feeling the worst, Alex came home. They were so happy to see her and couldn't get enough petting. Wherever Alex went, the kittens were right behind her.

Alex called her friend to tell her she was home and found out about the diarrhea and vomiting. Alex started looking around the house and found bloody vomit and bloody liquid stool on the sofa, floors, behind furniture and on the piano. She immediately called the vet and made an appointment for the following day. Tigger and Tassie would not eat nor would they eat their kitty treats which they loved.

The next morning, Alex put Tigger and Tassie in their carrier. They were so listless that they didn't meow on the way to the vet's office. "Your cats are both dehydrated," the vet told Alex. She ordered IV fluids to be given under their skin. Blood tests were done and the vet wanted to keep them overnight. "They have been through too much for me to leave them alone." Alex told the vet. It was agreed the cats could go home only if Alex went to the animal emergency room if there were any changes.

The vomiting and diarrhea persisted for another three days and then suddenly, the kittens were alert, active, hungry and wanted to play. "I will never leave you two alone again," Alex promised. And she didn't.

The kittens liked to eat early in the morning, around three or four o'clock. They devised a method to wake Alex for breakfast. Tigger would walk on Alex and if that didn't work, she started kneading her paws on Alex until she got up. Generally, this technique would work. The third method was for Tassie to lick Alex's hair and then pull it. This definitely got Alex's attention. These early hours weren't so frustrating to Alex except that the kittens went back to sleep once they were fed, and she was now awake and couldn't go back to sleep. In all reality, Alex didn't mind so much because she loved her little furry friends.

# Chapter Ten

"Did you just see what I saw?" Tigger meowed to Tassie.

"Do you mean the kitties that went by the window that looked just like Snowflake and Cotton Ball, all white fur with a black tipped tail?"

"Yes, only they were little like us when we were kittens. Come on, maybe we can see them from the bedroom window."

They went into the bedroom and jumped up on the bed to look out the window. Sure enough, there were two white kittens with black tails. With them was an adult cat that looked just like the kittens. Alex walked in just then. "Sweeties, these are feral cats just like you were when you were born. The difference is that you were rescued early and spent enough time with humans that you are now domesticated."

Tigger and Tassie saw something move and ran into the living room. There were six more kittens and a mom eating from a bowl. Alex came in the room and introduced them to more feral cats. With no one else to talk to, Alex explained to her cats that she had been feeding up to ten feral cats for about a year. "I don't know why you didn't notice before," she said. "Perhaps the kittens coming out for the first time made it possible for you to pay attention to them." Tigger and Tassie were excited but knew they would not be allowed outside to play with the kittens. In all actuality, it never would happen because as soon as the feral cats saw Tigger and Tassie, they ran. As time went on, the feral kittens grew and were bolder when Tigger and Tassie came to the screen door. At one point they were nose to nose through the screen. Alex had to stop the behavior because of the possibility of the feral cats spreading disease to her cats.

One day while Alex was doing the laundry she called to the cats. She had discovered a little brown field mouse and wanted to see what the kitties would do with it. Tigger and Tassie came into the laundry room and Alex showed them the mouse. The little mouse was scared and frozen in place and the cats had no clue what to do with it. First, they sniffed the mouse, then they pawed at it. Finally, the cats walked away and the mouse ran away. "Great white mouse hunters you are," Alex said laughing.

The cats loved watching birds and when they weren't perched on a window sill, they were in their cat tree watching the birds in the trees. Their favorite was a little green bird with a red top knot. The bird must have seen his own reflection in the glass because he repeatedly flew into the window hitting his head. The cats chirped and chirped at the bird. Of course, the bird couldn't hear the chirping nor could it see the cats. One day, the bird was gone and the cats actually went into a sort of mourning. They checked the window three or four times a day until they were sure the bird wasn't coming back. Several months later, the cats ran to investigate a thud sound. Sure enough, the bird had returned and resumed his head beating on the window.

And so, it went. Alex was content with her cats and they certainly were content being spoiled by their mom. Their personalities changed. Tassie was the aggressive cat and the one to get into trouble most often. Alex soon began to refer to her as her 'monster kitty.' This was an affectionate name and Tassie didn't mind. It was Tassie that broke two of Alex's expensive vases. "Well, I guess that was really my fault," Alex told Tassie. "After all you were only doing what kitties do and that is to climb."

Tigger, her shy kitty, came out of her shell and spent most of her waking hours following Alex around and looking for any opportunity to sit in her lap and be petted. Alex spent a lot of time on the computer with Tigger sitting in front of her. Tigger was part Main Coon and had a fabulous thick long tail that she flicked in Alex's face when sitting on her lap.

# Chapter Eleven

When the kittens were about eight months old, Alex decided to see how they would travel in the car. She promised them she would not leave them alone again and thought perhaps she could take the cats with her on a road trip. One sunny day, Alex introduced the cats to their new car carrier. It has a soft lining and gave the cats enough room to move around.

Tassie and Tigger were never leery of their carriers so getting them to go into the new one was not a problem. Alex had packed them food, water and a disposable litter box. The car was full of gas and Alex had packed a small bag for herself just in case the cats behaved well enough to make it an overnight trip.

Alex secured the carrier with the seat belt in the passenger side of the car in the front seat. The 'girls' as Alex had begun to refer to her two female cats, were quiet the first ten miles. Then Tigger began to meow intently. Tassie seemed to be fine with the ride, but Tigger began to try climbing out of the carrier. It was then that Alex did what no pet owner should do. She let Tigger out of the carrier. Tigger, who had the sweetest disposition, crawled into Alex's lap and watched the scenery. "You would think you were a puppy dog with the way you like to sit in my lap." Alex murmured to Tigger.

Alex and the kitties drove another three hours when Alex decided to see how Tigger and Tassie handled a motel room. Alex stopped in a small town and was able to get a pet friendly room. She unloaded the few belongings she brought for herself and the kittens. "OK girls, this is your home for tonight." In the room, she unzipped the carrier and the two cats bolted out looking for their litter box.

Alex took care in setting up the room for her girls. They had food, water and their litter box was situated away from their nourishment. Alex felt comfortable leaving them sleeping on the bed while she went out for dinner. An hour later, Alex returned to her motel room and when she opened the door, Tigger bolted out of the room. Alex was in a panic. It was dark and there was no way she could search outside for her beloved cat. She scouted the area around the motel room and called Tigger's name. Tigger did not respond and Alex was in a tizzy. She sat by the door outside with Tassie in her carrier next to her thinking Tigger would recognize the smell of either of them. After three hours, Alex took Tassie inside and they both curled up on the bed.

Alex didn't sleep well and dreamt of Tigger in the night frightened and not knowing what to do if she encountered a coyote or other animal. At four o'clock in the morning, Tassie woke up Alex. Alex sat up and heard a mournful meow. Knowing it was Tigger, she jumped out of bed and ran to the door. When she opened the door, Tigger was sitting in the corner of the building shaking. Alex picked her up and gave her hugs and kisses. "My precious kitty, where have you been?" she murmured in Tigger's fur. Tassie came over and the two kitties were nose to nose and then started their grooming routine. Alex knew all was well with the kitties but it would take a little longer for her to be okay.

Ten Years Later

For the past six months, Tigger was getting less adept at jumping onto counters. She also would walk several steps and then fall down. When she began to miss the litter box, Alex knew something was wrong. She took Tigger to the vet and she did spinal x-rays.

"Alex, Tigger has spinal stenosis. There is not much that can be done for her other than palliative treatment."

"What does that mean?"

"You can keep her comfortable and clean up after her when she misses the litter box. The other alternative is to put her down."

"I can't do that right now. Let me take her home and try to take care of her."

Now that Alex knew Tigger's problem, it became more and more difficult to take care of Tigger. Her symptoms rapidly grew worse and two weeks later Alex made a decision. She called the vet's office. "Hi, this is Tigger's mom and I need to bring her in." The receptionist asked why she wanted to bring Tigger in and Alex started crying. "I think it is time to put her down."

The receptionist was very kind and asked when it would be convenient for Alex to bring Tigger in. They agreed on a late appointment that afternoon. When Alex got to the vet's office, they didn't make her wait. She was escorted to a room with Tigger. They took Tigger out of her carrier and Alex held her. The vet came in and asked if Alex wanted to be with Tigger and Alex said that she did. While Alex held Tigger in her arms for the last time, the vet injected Tigger with a medication that stopped her heart. Within seconds, she was dead.

With tears running down her face, Alex medication that would end an animal's life. would otherwise suffer," the vet said.

Alex went home with a burning in her heart. For over ten years, Tigger had been a part of her life, along with Tassie. Tassie greeted Alex when she got home and she knew Tigger was not with Alex. There was no way Alex could explain what happened to Tigger and only hoped that they would both remember the joy Tigger gave both of them.

Ten Years Later

Tassie and Alex were nearly inseparable. Alex always suspected that Tassie missed her sister as much as she missed her. One morning when Tassie was fifteen years old, Alex didn't find her on the bed curled up as she always did in the morning. Alex got out of bed and went out to the kitchen. She searched the entire house and didn't find Tassie. She was beginning to worry when she found her beloved cat and companion in the laundry basket curled up in the dirty clothes. Tassie was still and Alex knew that she was no longer alive. Alex held Tassie for a while and then put her in a soft lined box and buried her in the back yard.

Alex cried and remembered when she first got Tigger and Tassie as kittens. They were so energetic and climbed on every piece of furniture they could find. They got Alex up early in the morning to eat and play. Their favorite toys were empty boxes and plastic shopping bags. There wasn't a morning that went by that they didn't watch the birds from the window sill. Alex was sure that they considered her one of their litter mates.

At the age of eighty, Alex was ready for her life to end and all she wanted was to join her little furry friends in the afterlife. On her last day on earth, she sat in her rocking chair and felt Tigger and Tassie sitting on her lap purring as she petted their fur.

*There can be no other love than that of a pet,*
*There can be no other comfort than that of a pet.*
*Pets are simply pure devotion and love,*
*Pets ask only that we give them care and love.*
*In return our pets are there for us,*
*When nothing else will help the void within us.*

# Just Charlie Knows

# Introduction

    Mom and I flew to Miami from Chicago for my grandmother's funeral three years ago. That was when we first noticed that grandpa had subtle tell-tale signs of forgetfulness. At first, we chalked it up to old age. Doesn't everyone lose their keys? However, each subsequent trip we made we became more concerned about the changes. They weren't big changes, but enough to alert us that grandpa's memory was beginning to be eaten away by Alzheimer's.

# Chapter One

Grandpa had a doctor's appointment and mom was trying to get him dressed and out of the house. "Darn, these buttons." Charlie muttered to no one in particular. It seems it was just last week that he could dress himself. Now he was a forgetful old man trying to get his shirt buttoned.

"Dad what are you muttering about?" Reggie asked.

"These gall durn buttons don't go through the hole. Must'a shrunk in the dryer. Mother always said that the sun is the best way to dry clothes."

"Here Dad. Let me help you." Reggie unbuttoned the buttons that were in unfamiliar button holes, straightened up his shirt and then systematically lined up the buttons and inserted them into the correct button holes one by one. "I have an idea. When we come back from your doctor's appointment, we'll stop and get you some pull over shirts. Then you won't need to worry about buttons."

"I've worn a buttoned shirt for the past sixty years. Why when I was working at the factory on airplanes, I worn a clean, white shirt and tie to go to work. These young kids today don't know a thing about lookin' nice. Here, why am I dressed in my good shirt?"

"Dad, you have a doctor's appointment. Remember we go to see Dr. George every month."

"Now why in tarnation do I need to see a doctor?"

Reggie knew it would do no good to explain to grandpa about

his progressing Alzheimer's disease. "Come on dad, or we'll be late."

Charlie dutifully followed Reggie from the bedroom into the kitchen. "Where's the coffee?" Charlie asked.

"Dad, we don't have time for coffee. I'll get you a cup when we get to the clinic."

"Why are we going to the clinic? I'm not sick."

"Let's go, dad."

On the way to see Dr. George, mom asked dad how the cleaning ladies were doing that we hired on our last trip. "I let 'em go. Seems they don't know how to clean and I can't understand half of what they are say'n to me. Besides, the house looks just fine."

"If you like mold growing in the toilet and algae in the kitchen sink and in the refrigerator," mom muttered. The remainder of the weekend mom and I cleaned grandpa's house. When we were finished, mom called the cleaning crew and reinstated them with the caveat that they were to call if grandpa dismissed them.

On Saturday, we were watching TV when the doorbell rang at five o'clock. "I'll get the door," I said wondering who it could be. When I opened the door there stood a little lady of about 4'10" with a mischievous grin and white hair. She was dressed much like a teenager with a short dress, leggings, a pony tail, tennis shoes and mismatched socks. "Well, hello. How can I help you?" I asked always the careful person with my foot in the door.

"Why, hello. Is Charlie home?"

"Yes, he is. And, who are you?"

"Oh, silly me. I'm Sunny and your father and I play poker every Saturday evening. Isn't that right, Honey'kins," she said peeking around me. At the sound of his nickname grandpa became alive and got out of his chair at lightning speed.

"Hello, Sunny," Grandpa said giving Sunny a big hug. He proceeded to introduce Sunny to mom and me without a glitch in memory loss. "Sunny and I play cards on Saturday evening."

"That's what Sunny said. What do you play, grandpa?"

"Well, you know it's just cards. What do we play, Sunny?"

"Poker and Hearts with some Gin Rummy thrown in." Grandpa had his arm around Sunny's waist. "We get in a little of that strip poker sometimes," grandpa gave Sunny a big smile. "Care to join us, ladies?"

Somewhat embarrassed and confused about a seventy-five-year old playing strip poker, we excused ourselves and grandpa and Sunny headed for the kitchen table and a round of cards. For the next two hours, mom and I listened as the "old" folks laughed and giggled.

"Mom, when we got here, we were going to talk to grandpa about setting him up in a memory home. But with Sunny, he seems to be somewhat normal."

"I know sweetheart. I have something I want to talk to you about."

"What's that, mom?"

"What would you think about moving from Chicago to Miami so we could be closer to dad? You will be out of high school this semester and on your way to Purdue in the fall."

"What about your job?"

"Before we left, I talked with the magazine editor and they are going to start a division of Glamour Anywhere in Miami in about six months. That would give us time to sell the condo and buy something here closer to grandpa."

"That's a lot to get done in six months. What about Dave?" Dave was a fellow mom had been dating for the past year. He was okay and he and mom seemed to have hit it off. So, what mom said next surprised me. "Honey, our relationship has been on the rocks for the past few months. He breaks more dates than he keeps and I suspect he is seeing someone else."

"Would you want to move and dump Dave?"

"Sweetie, dumping Dave is one of the reasons I want to move. I'm also weary of the cold, overcast climate in Chicago and would love to return to the beaches of Miami. What do you think of moving?"

"Works for me. I'd love to get a Florida tan before school starts in the fall."

"Perfect. Let's start a 'to do list' and get this ball rolling." Mom always did 'to do lists' when she was faced with multitasking. "We need to see how much money we can get for our condo. Fortunately, this is a good time for the housing market. Do you remember the square footage of the condo?" mom asked. I gave her my best guestimate of 2,000 square feet. Our condo was on the 33rd floor overlooking Lake Michigan. The view was magnificent and one that I would miss.

Mom continued with her list and as the hour got later, we realized that grandpa and Sunny were still in the kitchen. Or, at least we thought they were in the kitchen. As we searched the house for them, we heard soft snoring purrs from the family room. They were snuggled up together on the sofa, both fast asleep.

# Chapter Two

The following day, mom got ahold of Sunny and asked if she could talk with her before we left for home on the five o'clock flight to Chicago. "Mom, don't you think Sunny will tell grandpa about your conversation?"

"Probably, but she is the only one dad has here and I need to find out how much she thinks his memory is failing. Honey, why don't you take grandpa shopping while Sunny and I talk? We never did stop and get him his pull over shirts.

With a little coaxing, I persuaded grandpa to go to the shopping mall. "Grandpa, I need for you to stay with me while I look for some shirts for you." This order was like telling a two-year old not to toddle away. I was talking with the sales associate when I realized that grandpa was not with me. I asked if Security could do an over-head announcement to find grandpa. When grandpa didn't respond to the over-head page, the security guard called in another guard and we canvased the men's department to no avail. "We need to check the rest of the store," the guard commented. I headed for the ladies' lingerie department not expecting to find grandpa there. Well, I was in for a surprise when I saw grandpa holding up a lacey pair of panties.

"Grandpa, what are you looking at?" Grandpa looked up at me with his wonderful smile and sparkling green eyes. "I thought your grandmother would like these," grandpa said holding up the lacey panties.

"Grandpa, grandma died three years ago. Do you remember?"

"Well, of course I do," he said briskly. Mom and I had learned that grandpa tried to cover up his lapses in memory with anger, as if he was hiding the fact he couldn't remember.

"Come on, let's go back to the men's department and buy those shirts I was showing you." Grandpa went willingly and agreed to the blue, red, white and orange shirts. "I don't want those yellow and green shirts."

"Let's take a look at suspenders before we go," I suggested leading grandpa toward the belts and suspenders.

"Why would I want a couple of rubber bands keeping up my pants?"

I needed to be careful in what I said next. "Grandpa, your belts are getting hard for you to buckle up. Remember, they have little holes you have to find, just like the button holes on your shirts. Besides, suspenders are very fashionable these days. Don't you think Sunny would like suspenders?"

"By golly, that just might be a fine idea." And, so we bought two pair of suspenders. Grandpa wore the red pair home.

# Chapter Three

When we got home, grandpa laid down for his afternoon nap. Mom got home shortly thereafter. We grabbed a couple of sodas from the refrigerator and went out on the deck where there was a perfect spring breeze and a view of the ocean. My grandparents bought their two-bedroom home back in the 1940's. It was located on the beach and had been a target of realtors for many years. Grandpa had added on to the house over the years so that it was now three bedrooms and a family room. He also vowed that he would never sell the property and specified in his will that neither my mom, nor myself could sell any part of it.

"How was the day with grandpa?" Mom asked taking a long drink of her soda.

"How does spending the day with a two-year old sound?" We both laughed and then I told mom about my escapade with grandpa at the department store. "Mom, I don't think grandpa should be living alone."

"I would agree with you. However, I can't get out here much earlier than we planned and you've got the rest of the school year to finish."

"What about a live-in person? I don't know if he needs a nurse right now, but he certainly needs someone to look after him."

"Sally, I totally agree. I don't know what your grandfather will think of the idea."

"Is there a way we can stay longer to figure something out?

"You have another week of spring break and I can get a week's leave from work. It would give us more time to observe your grandfather and perhaps find a live-in nurse, or person."

"Mom, I almost forgot. How was your visit with Sunny?"

"Sunny is a delightful person. I learned that she is seventy years old and has been a widow for the past five years. Her husband was some high-ranking officer in the Navy and she is enjoying his generous pension. It was a relief to learn that she won't be after dad's money. She was a Navy nurse and they traveled the world together. They have no children and her brother and sister have passed away. So, in essence dad and Sunny have each other."

"How did they meet?"

"Of all places, in the grocery store. Dad was in the produce department muttering something about not knowing how to cook vegetables. Sunny walked up and joined in dad's monologue and they got to talking. Before she knew it, Dad had asked her over for a glass of wine and a game of cards."

"Wasn't that a bit bold to ask a stranger over the first time they met?"

"I suppose so, however, Sunny looks so kind and dad seems to resemble a small child in his actions these days. Neither one looks like a serial killer."

"OK, then what happened?"

"Sunny accepted his invitation and she was on his doorstep at five o'clock sharp. She said she brought a bottle of wine and it was a good thing because dad didn't have any wine in the house."

"What does she say about grandpa's memory?"

"I asked her about that and she said that his memory is worse than it was when they met. Now, what is interesting is that he can remember the cards that have been played when they play poker."

"But he can't remember what he had for breakfast."

"Correct."

"If we are going to stay for another week, let's invite Sunny to go on an outing and we can see if grandpa is any different with her."

"Great idea, Sally. Let's see if she wants to go for a walk on the beach tomorrow and then have lunch at the Sand and Ocean restaurant which is one of dad's favorites. I'll give Sunny a call.

# Chapter Four

Sunny was delighted to join us the following day for a walk on the beach. Dad dressed in his favorite Hawaiian flowered shorts, one of his new pull-over shirts and his red suspenders. At 5'10" and his tousled brown hair, he looked as adorable as the child he was becoming. Sunny was decked out in a pair of jean shorts with lace sewn on the bottom, a frilly lace top and a very large Sombrero straw hat. As they walked hand in hand ahead of us mom and I smiled at each other relishing in the fact that grandpa had found happiness again.

We walked for about an hour along the shoreline. Grandpa and Sunny had taken off their shoes by this time and walked in the waves up to their knees. Observing grandpa for any physical problems, he appeared to have a steady gait. He and Sunny picked up seashells, ran after each other in the incoming waves and looked like a couple many years younger.

"Let's catch up with your grandfather and Sunny. The restaurant is just up ahead."

Much to our disappointment, when we caught up with grandpa he asked mom, "Do I know you?"

"Dad, its Reggie, your daughter."

Sunny took dad's hand and told us that he would be okay in a few minutes. "Let me get a table and then you can join us."

Sunny was correct. She and grandpa sat down at a table by

the window and when we walked up, Sunny clapped her hands and looking at grandpa, she said, "Honey-kin's, look who is here to have lunch with us."

"By golly, it's Reggie and Sally. Where did you come from?"

On the walk home, mom and I talked about some strategies to get grandpa some care until we could get moved to Miami.

"What do you think grandpa will say when we suggest a live-in?" I asked.

Mom laughed. "He will be furious and insulted. But, he'll get over it. I'd also like to meet with Dr. George, his neurologist, and see what she has to suggest."

We spent the rest of the walk home in silence. Mom walked in the waves and we both watched the seagulls taking flight on gusts of wind diving for their dinner.

# Chapter Five

Mom got an appointment with Dr. George on Tuesday after hours. She seemed only too happy to see us and talk about grandpa's condition. I told her about our shopping event and our concern about his failing memory.

"Let's talk about Charlie's medical history since he has been a patient of mine. I first saw Charlie when his wife, Gina, brought him in five years ago. She was concerned about his inability to find his keys and glasses. Knowing that we all have this forgetfulness when we get into our sixties and seventies, I told her to watch Charlie and keep a diary of her concerns. She was diligent about writing down what she observed."

"Over the next two years, he was no longer able to do table top puzzles. This is important because it is an inability to work in a spatial field. In other words, Charlie couldn't determine the size and color of puzzle pieces. He became more confused keeping track of the time during the day, but more importantly, he didn't always know where he was."

"When Gina got sick and died, Charlie became more confused. That was about the time he met Sunny who has been wonderful for Charlie. She probably told you they play cards on Saturday afternoons. Well, she visits Charlie every day and makes sure he has food and has eaten his meals. Sunny has told me that she would watch out for Charlie, but that she doesn't want to be a live-in girlfriend." We all laughed at Dr. George's last statement.

A couple of months ago, Sunny found Charlie putting up a Christmas tree. This is might not be significant if it hadn't been for the fact that he was on a ten-foot ladder stringing lights on top of the tree in July. Two weeks before that, Sunny couldn't find Charlie in the house. She called the police and they found him three blocks away sitting on a bench. He had been crying because he didn't know how to get back home."

"It would be helpful if you could find a live-in to watch over Charlie, the Sargent at the sign in desk at the police station stated. We have information at the front desk about services who provide twenty-four-hour care to those with Alzheimer's."

We thanked Dr. George for her time and picked up some brochures on the way out. "We need to interview some of these agencies," mom said as we walked to the car. "Do you think we could split the list and we can both do the interviewing?"

"That would be fine. We should call and get the interviews set up ASAP because we'll be going home in a couple of days and I would like to know grandpa is being looked after."

Going down the list of agencies on the way home, I counted ten that provided 24/7 care. I called the first name and explained our situation with grandpa and our crunch on time. The director was very helpful and we set up an interview for ten o'clock the next morning. I had called three more agencies by the time we got home and set up appointments. After we returned home, Mom did the same thing with her list and found three of her agencies could accommodate grandpa.

The next morning, mom and I were up early and made a list of questions we wanted answered in the interviews. Naturally, we wanted to know their experience with the memory impaired. What would he/she do if grandpa got combative? Was he/she available 24/7? Did he/she provide house cleaning, cooking and laundry? Did he/she have transportation? Would he/she be willing to take grandpa on outings? We planned to tell the candidates about Sunny and how important she would be to Charlie's life. Did they have a problem with Sunny coming over each day?

When we got to the first interview place, Memory Lane, we met with the director of the program. Mom and I were disappointed because we thought we would be meeting with the caregiver. We asked the director our questions and told her if we chose their agency, we wanted to come back and meet the caregiver that would be selected for grandpa. We had the same experience with the second agency.

"Sally, let's go somewhere for a nice lunch."

"Great idea. The Steak and Brew is a block away and the food is good." Mom pulled out of the parking lot and drove to the restaurant. We asked for a quiet booth, but that was like asking for a quiet bleacher at a football game. "What did you think of the first two places?" I asked mom as we were seated.

"It is going to be a tough call and I don't think we are going to know until we get someone and Charlie allows them in the house. That's the other problem, Sally. We need to be around for a few days to make sure that Charlie will accept this new person."

"Are you thinking that we should choose someone from today and get them to start tomorrow or the next day?"

"If we can pull it off, that would be the best plan."

We each had a delicious salad for lunch and mom had a glass of wine. "Let's go see how the next two agencies are."

The third place was a mirror of the morning interviews. When we got to A Last Stop, we wondered what we would find with such a name. We walked into a luxurious living room. There were residents playing cards, watching television and playing pool. Off to the side was a coffee bar with an expresso machine and pastries. A nice woman at the front desk asked if we needed help. We told her we had an appointment at three o'clock with Stephanie. "That would be our in-house caregiver coordinator. I'll call her and let her know you are here."

"Hmm. We aren't meeting with the director," mom whispered to me.

Within two minutes a pretty young woman in her thirties came through the locked door and walked over to us. "Hi, Reggie and Sally, I'm Stephanie and the coordinator of the in-house caregiver program. Shall we go to my office?" Mom and I immediately felt at ease with Stephanie and the surroundings. We explained grandpa's situation and that we were going to be moving to Miami within the next few months. "Now that I know a little bit more about Charlie, I would like to call in Cindy who would be assigned to Charlie should you choose our services?" Stephanie made a short phone call and Cindy walked into the room as soon as Stephanie hung up the phone. Cindy was young, perhaps thirty years old. She pulled her long blonde hair back into a pony tail, wore little make up and had a charming personality. "Cindy is our star caregiver and I think she and Charlie would get along famously."

Cindy gave us one of her five-million-dollar smiles and sat down across from us. We asked her our questions and were impressed with her answers for such a young person. "What would you do if Charlie became combative?" Cindy put on her serious face and told us that she would wait until his anger had dissipated making sure he, or anyone else, wasn't hurt. "You know, Reggie and Sally, Alzheimer's patients get angry or combative because they are frightened, or don't understand why they can't remember something very simple. They become like little frightened children and it is our job to be there for them. They should never be in a situation where they might feel they are abandoned."

We knew Cindy was our girl and asked if she could start in the morning. "Cindy is between assignments so she would be available to start tomorrow with Charlie." Stephanie reassured us.

We were both smiling when we left to drive home. "Who is going to tell grandpa?"

"I would think we both should and we need to do it tonight."

When we visited grandpa, mom took one bedroom and I took the other. "We should give the larger of the two bedrooms to Cindy while we are still here. That means, mom, you are on the sofa."

Mom laughed, "I can do that for a couple of nights if I know things will work out between Charlie and Cindy. In the meantime, you can help me clean out my bedroom so Cindy feels welcome tomorrow. Then, we need to talk to dad."

By the time we finished picking up mom's stuff and spit polishing the bedroom for Cindy it was early evening and we still needed to talk with grandpa. "Mom, let's order a pizza and maybe we can start our talk with grandpa over dinner."

"It's not going to be easy to talk with Charlie, but go ahead and order the pizza and I'll set the table." We hadn't seen grandpa for an hour or so, but we weren't worried about him.

When we left the bedroom, we heard the television blaring. "Grandpa, I yelled. Turn that thing down." Just then Sunny came out of the TV room smiling. "Don't worry, Sally, Charlie's asleep and can't hear a thing." Sunny was her adorable self in a denim jump suit with a ruffled shirt and her hair tied back with a brightly colored scarf.

"Actually, we're glad to have a chance to talk with you alone, mom said. "Sally and I came to a decision yesterday that Charlie needs care at home day and night. We know that you come over to see him, but we think he needs more attention than that." I noticed that Sunny was listening to mom intently and waited until mom was finished talking. "Sally and I interviewed caregivers today and a delightful young lady will move in tomorrow morning and will be with Charlie 24/7. Except, of course, when you and Charlie are together. Sally and I had planned to talk with Charlie after dinner. Would you like to be present?"

Sunny continued to look at us and we weren't sure if she was in agreement with the decision mom and I made. Slowly that charming smile grew on her face. She stepped forward and on her tip toes, she gave each of us a hug and a kiss on the cheek. "I have been so worried about Charlie. I didn't want to say anything because I wanted you to make up your own minds as to when Charlie needed in-house care. You know I love him dearly, but I can't take care of him at my age. Yes, I would love to stay when you talk to Charlie tonight."

Mom and I were delighted with what Sunny had to say and now felt we should have included Sunny in our decision. Thirty minutes later a young and very good-looking pizza delivery boy came. Mom paid him and gave him a generous tip, something about not having any change. Sunny woke up grandpa twenty minutes earlier and he was hungry as a bear, or so he told us. Dinner was pleasant and after we cleared away the paper boxes and plates, mom and I looked at each other. Mom nodded at me that it was time to start talking with grandpa.

"Dad, Sally and I are concerned about you living alone and your safety. The house has not been cleaned and there is no food in the refrigerator. We don't even know who does your laundry."

Grandpa looked at mom and me and with a tear in his eye he looked at the floor. "Grandpa?" I went over and knelt by his chair. "Grandpa, we want to talk to you about someone staying with you."

"Sunny takes good care of me, don't you Sunny?" All eyes were on Sunny and she said with tears in her eyes, "Yes, Charlie, I do what I can but I'm an old lady and I can't care for you and me day and night. I'd like for you to listen to what Reggie and Sally have to say."

Now Charlie was crying. He took Sally's hand and asked, "Will you and your mother still come to visit me?" We all laughed and Charlie laughed with us not knowing why.

"Dad, Sally and I are going to move to Miami so that we can be closer to you. We figure it will take about six months to sell the condo in Chicago and get moved to Miami. In the meantime, Cindy will be here and will take good care of you."

"Who is Cindy?" he asked.

"The young lady who is a care-giver and will be staying with you."

"Come on Sunny, let's play cards. Maybe even a little strip poker." Charlie and Sunny got up. Charlie took Sunny's hand and they went to the kitchen to play cards.

"That went better than I expected," mom said. "What did you think?"

"Actually, I think we're still in for the storm when grandpa realizes he will have someone living with him."

"You're probably right. I am so tired that I could fall asleep on my feet. I am claiming the sofa. Would you say goodnight to the poker playing couple. I will see you in the morning."

"Night, mom. I love you."

"I love you too sweetie."

# Chapter Six

The next morning mom and I were up early in anticipation of Cindy's arrival at nine o'clock. We had grandpa out of bed at eight and coaxed him to shower, shave and put on one of his new shirts. He promptly spilled orange juice and a few minutes before nine we were changing his shirt. Things were happening so quickly Charlie had little time to wonder what was going on.

Promptly at nine o'clock, the doorbell rang and Cindy was standing there with her huge smile. We could feel her energy spilling into the room. Cindy sort of floated into the living room and was at grandpa's side. She knelt on the floor and looking at grandpa with a warm smile said, "Hi, my name is Cindy."

Grandpa looked at her with a quizzical expression. "What are you doing here?"

Cindy's smile got even bigger. "I am your new live-in friend."

I looked at mom as we watched this scenario play out.

"I know that Sunny is your girlfriend, but I want to be your friend too. What do you think about that?"

Just then Sunny walked in. Cindy was obviously intrigued by Sunny's attire of plaid pants and a striped shirt. Cindy got off the floor and introduced herself to Sunny. "Charlie and I have decided to be friends. Shall we include you in our little friend group?"

Sunny quickly picked up on Cindy's energy. "A friendship group of three. Do you play poker?"

Both Cindy and Sunny had the rest of us laughing within minutes. Grandpa looked happy and comfortable. Mom winked at me and I knew we were both thinking the same thing. We made a great decision and hoped that it would last once we left for Chicago.

Cindy wasn't in a hurry to bring in her personal belongings. She spent the morning getting to know grandpa and the relationship he had with Sunny. Grandpa showed her his bedroom and a photo album from his teens and young adult years which he had never shared with mom and me. Next, they went outside to see grandpa's 1950 Pontiac convertible that he bought when it was new. They sat in the front seat with the top down. When I took them glasses of lemonade grandpa was telling Cindy stories of when he was a young man and took young ladies to the drive-in theatre in the convertible. Mom and I had taken the car keys away from grandpa a year earlier, so there was no danger in them driving off. When I went inside, I told mom about the story grandpa was telling Cindy.

She smiled and gave me a hug. "We can go home now with peace of mind with Cindy here."

Grandpa took a nap after lunch and we had a chance to talk with Cindy. "Well, what do you think?" mom asked her.

"Your father is adorable and I do believe we will get on famously. Right now, he is comfortable because you and Sally are here and he feels safe. This is Tuesday and you are going back to Chicago Sunday morning. Right?" We nodded in agreement.

"I would like to try something before you leave to see how Charlie is when you are not here. I would like to take him on an outing tomorrow to see how he reacts in a crowd. I am asking that you both stay home, or spend the day shopping. Without you, he is going to lose his security blanket. So that will be Wednesday. On Thursday, I am going to ask you, Reggie and Sally, to pack up and get a hotel room for a couple of days. You can come over and visit with Charlie, but he needs to be comfortable with the two of us in the house together."

Mom and I looked at each other and didn't say anything. "If you suddenly leave Sunday morning without a weaning time, Charlie is going to feel abandoned and neither Sunny nor I will be able to console him."

"Cindy, I am sure the reason Sally and I have nothing to say is that we don't know what to say. Surely, we would have left Sunday morning and would have expected dad to understand we were going home. How frightened he would have been."

I waited for mom to finish and then asked Cindy how she was so knowledgeable about Alzheimer's at her early age.

"I get asked that a lot by my client's families." Cindy took a deep breath and settled back in the over-stuffed chair. I am thirty years old and have lost my parents and grandparents to early onset Alzheimer's. I also have aunts and uncles who have early onset Alzheimer's." Cindy took a deep breath and sipped on her lemonade.

"When my parents were young, there was no testing and most of the old folks were diagnosed with dementia or chronic brain syndrome. When their parents, or my grandparents, died we accepted their death as natural causes."

"I was thirteen when my mother began to forget where she put her car keys and reading glasses. She was thirty years old at the time. I learned very early in life how to keep house and took on the role of parent as my mother became more and more debilitated. By the time I was eighteen, my dad showed the same signs of memory loss as my mom. You can imagine how devastated I was when I found out I would be caring for my parents for what seemed like forever. My childhood had been taken from me and now my adult years would be taken. My mother died when I was twenty-three which would have made her forty years old. My father was inconsolable when mom died and he died two years later. I was twenty-five years old and didn't have a career or any money. My parents were unable to work and we received money from the state."

We knew Cindy had told her story before and waited for her

to continue.

"I ended up on the street for a year. Luckily, I never got into the drug scene but it was difficult to escape it. One day, I was sleeping in front of St. Luke's Catholic Church when a priest saw me. He woke me up and asked why I was sleeping on the steps. I told him I didn't have a place to stay and didn't have any money. My clothes were in taters and my face and hands were encrusted with dirt. He asked me if I was hungry and my eyes got huge as I shook my head yes. He took me by the hand and led me to the rectory where he and several other priests lived. I was given a marvelous bowl of stew which I can still taste if I close my eyes. The priest asked how I came to be on the street and I told him my story. By this time, all of the priests were listening to me. They laughed at my stories and antics. It was then that I realized no matter how far down you get, laughter will always get you out of the doldrums."

"How long did you stay with the priests?"

"As luck would have it, the priest's live-in maid had just retired and they had not decided on a replacement from the stack of applications they had. The next day, after a hot bath and some hand me down clothes, not to mention a couple of hot meals in my stomach, they offered me the job. I was used to hard work and loved the humor of the priests. Not many people know how funny a priest can be and they are not as holy and righteous as they want us to think they are. It was the priests that taught me how to laugh and how to spread that laughter to others. When I left, I had decided to work with the memory impaired. I had plenty of experience, love and acceptance that I could give to all of my patients. I also understand about their fears, fear of the unknown, fear of being abandoned and fear of dying. The memory impaired can't remember what they did for a living and for so many people, their careers identified who they were. Can you imagine being frightened all of the time? That's why consistency is very important in their lives."

"By the way, I want to know more about Charlie, his life and what he did for a living. But for now, I would like to get settled in before Charlie wakes up. And, I would like for Charlie to be part of our next conversation this evening. If you have photos of his earlier years, that would be helpful. Be selective so that he doesn't get overwhelmed."

# Chapter Seven

I was eighteen years old and had a wonderful mother. Cindy was my age when her mom started demonstrating symptoms of Alzheimer's. I was reflecting on this as I laid on my bed and mom came in. "Cindy is a remarkable young woman," she said sitting on the side of the bed.

"Mom, tell me about my dad." Mom didn't say anything. She stared at the floor. "Did he really leave you when I was born?"

"Sweetie, it's time to tell you the whole story of me and your father. Your father didn't leave me, I left him. Jason and I met in high school. He was this sexy football player that all of the girls were after. I was okay looking, but as with most young girls I hated my body and thought I was ugly. It didn't help being an only child and your grandparents were very protective of me."

"I was a junior in high school which made me sixteen years old. At the end of the school year, there was a beach party with a big bon fire and lots of beer. I begged my parents to let me go. We argued and I got grounded. The party wasn't far from the house and I managed to sneak out and join my classmates. Jason was there and he was the center of attention with the girls. I had no experience with beer, let alone with boys. The music got louder, the beer flowed heavier and I found myself dancing with Jason. I was floating high on excitement as we danced. By this time, some of the boys brought out hard liquor. It tasted nasty but I managed to get some of it down."

"Jason convinced me to walk down the beach to the yacht club. He told me his dad had a yacht and we could go and star gaze. Not knowing what to say or how to get out of the situation, I followed him. When he wasn't sure what yacht we should get into, I should have known he was full of crap and his father did not own a boat. Anyway, we found a boat with chairs on the deck. Now it started to get scary."

"Jason began looking for liquor and broke into the liquor cabinet. I asked him to take me back to the party and, of course, he refused. He told me a pack of lies about how pretty and smart I was and then we started making out. I don't know how long we made out before I realized he was taking my clothes off. His clothes were already off. I now know that Jason date raped me."

"I somehow managed to get back to the party and home where I sneaked into my bedroom through the window. Mom heard me coming in and met me. She quizzed me about where I had been, who I was with and what I was doing. All I could tell her was I went to the party and had a beer. I thought I had her convinced about my story, but you know, darling, mothers know all. Mom kissed me goodnight and tucked me under the covers."

"Two months later, I had missed two periods. Mom knew because the Kotex pads had not been used for two months. She came into my bedroom one day and sat down. She asked if we could talk. After a pause, she asked what happened at the beach party. I immediately started to cry big crocodile tears and threw myself down on the bed. Mom kept rubbing my back and waited for me to stop crying. She asked again what happened at the party. I was a little girl curled up in her lap crying and telling her about that night. She asked if I thought I was pregnant. I told her I had missed two periods."

"Were you pregnant?"

"Yes. Mom took me to a doctor in another town and he confirmed

I was pregnant. There was no choice of abortion in those days and mom took me with her when she talked to Jason's mother. Jason denied what happened. It was his word against mine."

"I had to drop out of school and was the black sheep of the town. I was very depressed during my pregnancy but mother and dad were always there for me. Jason and I started going out and we thought we had fallen in love. We were married a month before you were born. What a beautiful baby you were and I thought I had started a new life with you and Jason."

"I enrolled in school to finish my senior year. Jason was a year older and he joined the Navy two months after you were born. He was so handsome in his uniform and was anxious to go overseas. We wrote letters every week in the beginning, then he wrote less and less. His first tour of duty lasted six months in Hawaii. When we came home, he was home for another six months before he went out to sea. He must have had a wonderful time in Hawaii because he gave me a good dose of syphilis."

"Oh, my God," I gasped.

"Jason went through all of the mea culpas and said he would never stray again. I believed him and he went off to Japan for his next tour of duty and was gone a year. This time when he returned home, he had a wife and baby with him."

"How could that be?"

"It is very simple. Jason couldn't keep it in his pants and the Japanese women are beautiful when they are young. They also will do almost anything to get to the States. I reported him to the military authorities and he was arrested and his wife and child sent back to Japan. He spent a year in the brig and when he got out, he was street smart. He knew how to buy and sell drugs, he extorted women, and he stole cars and resold them for big money. He basically became part of the underground."

"During the time he was in the brig, I started divorce proceedings. Even though Jason was the bad guy and I was the culprit, it was a painful process. I was twenty years old with a two-year old and no education or job. Mom and dad offered to send me to college. This was to be a one-time deal. If I dropped out for any reason, they would not extend college support to me in any terms. I enrolled in the local community college my first two years. They had a day care, so I could leave you in a safe place. Then as you know I transferred to San Francisco and finished up my degree in fashion design."

"What happened to dad?"

"Two months after he was released from prison, he was accosted in a dark alley by some street gang guys that had been in prison with him. They beat him to death with Billy clubs. When the paramedics got there, it apparently looked like a war zone. Jason was pronounced dead at the scene."

"That must have been awful for you."

"Darling, I would do it again if it meant having another daughter as wonderful as you are. Now, it's time for dad to get up from his nap and for him and Cindy to continue getting acquainted."

# Chapter Eight

Grandpa usually slept for two hours after lunch and he wandered out of his bedroom at three o'clock. Cindy had put her things in her bedroom, but brought out a few of her belongings into the living room and TV room to indicate that she was living there and had established her territory. One of the items was an overstuffed brown dog with long floppy ears. Grandpa was immediately attracted to the dog, picked it up and went back to his chair.

"That's Dooley," Cindy told grandpa. "He goes everywhere with me and likes to be held and petted."

Grandpa didn't say anything, just petted Dooley.

Cindy turned to mom and me. "I always bring a new stuffed animal with me. Clients will identify with the childlike feelings it brings out. In this case, Charlie is looking for security."

"Charlie, would you like to rename Dooley?" Cindy was engaging Charlie in transferring ownership of Dooley to him. "Oh, no. I like Dooley. Do you want him back now?"

"No Charlie, I think Dooley likes you and you can keep him."

Charlie and Cindy chatted for a while. Mom and I were in the kitchen discussing the uniqueness of Cindy's approach when we heard grandpa talking about his job working on Navy jets as a mechanic. "Come on, Sally, let's go join them."

"By golly, you should have seen those jet engines. It was the biggest thing the Navy had to get those planes off the ground."

"Where did you work on the jet engines?" Charlie stopped and looked at Cindy. "Well, at North Island. Where do you think I worked on the jets?"

"Do you have any pictures of yourself when you were younger? I'll bet you were a handsome young man." Cindy was coaxing the conversation back to grandpa.

"Dad, isn't this your photo album?"

"Where did you get that? That's mine." Charlie asked Reggie abruptly.

"I know Dad, but Cindy asked to see pictures of you when you were younger."

"Oh, that's different." Grandpa took the album from mother's outstretched hand. Cindy went over and sat next to Charlie on the sofa. Grandpa was going back in time and we gave him the time he needed to find himself.

"These were the jets the Navy pilots used to fly during the war. See these guys next to the plane, they were all mechanics like me."

"Were you in the war, grandpa?"

"Nope. I was too old for World War Two and too young for the Vietnam War. So, I did the next best thing I could and that was to work on jets."

We spent the next hour going through pictures neither my mom nor I had ever seen. There were group pictures of dad's working buddies, some taken at the beach and included pretty women. "Look grandpa, there you are with your 1950 Pontiac."

"Cindy, did I show you my red Pontiac?"

"No, Charlie. I don't believe you did. Shall we look at it and maybe take a ride?"

Grandpa and Cindy went outside. When mom and I looked out the kitchen window, grandpa had on his beret hat. Cindy was pointing at objects in the yard and grandpa was laughing as he turned the steering wheel back and forth.

Sunny came over for the evening and Cindy joined her and

grandpa in a game of poker. We were sure Cindy knew the rules of the game. However, she engaged Charlie in explaining how to play. Later Cindy commented on grandpa's ability to keep track of the cards played. "He has always been able to do that, even before he started forgetting things," mom replied.

After Sunny left, Cindy told Charlie that they, the two of them, would be going to the zoo in the morning. "Why would we do that?" he asked. Cindy laughed which caused grandpa to laugh. "Because I want to see the animals and would like you to show them to me."

"Well, in that case we should go. Are you ready?"

"Charlie, it is dark outside and the animals are asleep. How about we go after breakfast?"

"Can Dooley go too?"

"We can talk about that in the morning. Now it is time for you to get ready for bed. If you need any help, just give me a holler." Like a dutiful child, Charlie headed off to his bedroom.

"How do you do that?" mom asked.

"You have to give them as much freedom as is safe. Charlie is capable at this time of getting himself ready for bed and needs to have the dignity of doing it alone."

# Chapter Nine

Charlie was up and dressed, well sort of dressed, by seven o'clock the next morning. He had Dooley under his arm and his hat and sunglasses on. "Charlie, where are you going?" Cindy looked up from her cup of coffee.

"To the zoo," Charlie said with a big grin.

"I am so happy that you remembered where we are going this morning. We need to have breakfast first and wait for the animals to wake up. Charlie, you also need to finish getting dressed." It was then we all realized Charlie didn't have on his shorts. Here, Charlie, have a seat next to me and then you can find your shorts after you eat."

After breakfast, Cindy suggested to Charlie that they spend a little time re-buttoning his shirt. "You know Charlie, it took me a long time to learn how to button a shirt. Let's do it together."

"Mom, we fought with grandpa every morning to get his shirt buttoned straight. Cindy has him wrapped around her little finger."

"Not really." Cindy smiled. Another thing with the memory impaired is not to blame or to tell them they are wrong. Charlie wants to please and often times he doesn't know how."

An hour later, Cindy and grandpa were ready to leave for the zoo. "Alright ladies, Charlie and I are off and you are on your own today. Go to lunch, go shopping and have fun. Don't forget to book a hotel room for Thursday and Friday nights.

The Miami Zoo covers many acres and I knew grandpa and Cindy would be gone for most of the day. I cleaned up the breakfast dishes and mom made some phone calls to her boss. We were showered and dressed by noon and ready to hit the shopping malls. I thought we would shop all of the store fronts, but we found we were walking up and down the mall.

"I am in no mood to shop. Let's scout out the hotels and book a room for the next two nights," mom offered.

We drove to the beach towns and found a cottage style motel on the shoreline and we booked a cottage room for Thursday, Friday and Saturday nights. We spent the afternoon walking on the beach and sitting on the deck talking.

"Mom, I have been thinking. I want to change my declared major when I go to college next year."

"Why? What made you change your mind? You have wanted to be a dental hygienist for as long as I can remember."

"I know, but spending this week with grandpa and meeting Cindy has made me think how I can do something good for the world. Keeping people's teeth in good condition is important, but I'd like to make a difference in people's lives."

"What are you thinking of studying?"

"I would like to look into being a social worker and help people like grandpa get matched up with experts like Cindy. Mom, I can see such a difference in grandpa since Cindy arrived just yesterday."

"That would be a marvelous career path and you would be good at it. Why don't you find out if Purdue has a social worker degree program? If not, then you'll have to hustle to find a school and get accepted in the next few months."

"Thanks, mom. I had hoped you would understand."

"Sweetie, you know I will support your career goals."

# Chapter Ten

Cindy and grandpa returned from the zoo late afternoon. Grandpa was elated and exhausted at the same time. "A nap would certainly feel good right now," Cindy said looking at grandpa.

"Say, now. That is a great idea," grandpa said as he headed for the bedroom.

"You did it again, Cindy," mom said.

"Another memory tip is to make a suggestion that the patient thinks it's his idea. You get a lot more accomplished that way."

"How was the zoo?" Mom asked.

"It was a fun day. Your father showed me his favorite animals and I think we saw the monkeys at least four times." We all laughed. "Charlie was very well behaved and didn't wander off at any time. What I learned is that he needs the stimulation of outings."

"How was your day shopping?" Cindy inquired.

"We didn't do any shopping. We did find a delightful cottage motel on the beach and spent the day relaxing."

"Perfect. Do you have your bags packed? I would like you to be here when Charlie wakes up, say goodbye and then leave Charlie with me."

"Okay. Our bags are packed. Sally, could you put them in the car."

It all seemed strange having Cindy take over the role of caregiver. Wasn't that what mom and I were supposed to do? Twenty minutes after I returned from the car, Charlie had gotten up from his nap.

"Dad, Sally and I are going to spend the night at a motel on the beach. You'll be okay with Cindy and she can call anytime you need us."

"I am going to teach Cindy how to play strip poker," Charlie said with a twinkle in his eye.

"We'll see about that, Charlie," Cindy said putting her arm around Charlie's shoulders.

Mom and I walked to the car not saying anything. "Are you okay?" I asked as we drove away.

"I honestly don't know. I am his daughter and feel as though I have relinquished my duties to a stranger."

I reached over and squeezed her arm. "Mom, think of it as doing what is best for grandpa. We can't be there for him when we are in Chicago and we can't take him to Chicago with us. He will be just fine."

"Thanks, sweetie."

# Chapter Eleven

The remainder of the week went without a hitch. We spent time with Cindy, Charlie and Sunny and still gave Cindy time alone with grandpa. Sunday morning, we turned in our rental car at the airport. We had said our goodbyes at the house and looked forward to getting home and back into our routines.

I researched social worker degrees at Purdue and was delighted to learn that there were several tracks in their social worker program. The best part was not having to apply to another university and try to get accepted with such a short time frame. I contacted a counselor and changed my declared major.

Mom didn't waste any time, either. She got in touch with a realtor and put our condo up for sale. Her next task as to talk with her boss about a transfer to Miami. Glamour Anywhere was still scheduled to open its office in Miami and mom was able to talk her boss into working from home in Miami until the office opened. It all seemed to fall into place and we only needed to sell the condo.

We talked on a conference call each evening with Cindy and grandpa. They seemed to be getting along famously and we didn't worry about them.

A month after we were home, mom got a call from Sunny. "Reggie, something terrible has happened."

"Sunny, what's wrong?" Mom asked waving to me to listen in on the conversation.

"Charlie and Cindy were out for a walk when a car swerved and hit Cindy. She is in the hospital and in pretty bad shape."

"Where's Charlie?"

"Charlie's home and I am staying with him but I can't do it alone much longer. Can you and Sally come to Miami right away?"

"Of course, Sunny. I will call you back with our flight arrangements."

"Did you hear, Sally? We need to return to Miami. I will call for tickets and hope we can leave tonight."

"Mom, I've got mid-terms next week that I need to study for."

"Could you come with me for a couple of days?"

"Of course." I said giving mom a big hug.

We both packed a carry-on suitcase and mom got tickets that would get us in late afternoon. She called Sunny and told her we would get a rental car and be at the house by early evening.

When we got to the house, Sunny greeted us with red-rimmed eyes. "I am so glad you are here. I didn't know what to do."

"Thank you for calling us, Sunny. Can we ask you to stay with Charlie for a couple more hours? I want to go to the hospital and see Cindy before I talk with Charlie."

"Yes, Reggie I can but don't be too long."

Mom and I made record time getting to the hospital. Despite the HIPPA laws, we managed to find out that Cindy was in the Surgical Critical Care Unit. Mom convinced the nurses that she was Cindy' only relative, her aunt and I was her niece. Cindy's nurse escorted us to her private room.

We were shocked to find Cindy on a respirator with a breathing tube in her nose, three IV's, a chest tube in her chest attached to a plastic container on the floor. Her face was black and blue and she had a huge bandage around her head and a tube from her head to a machine that monitored her cranial pressure.

"My God, what happened to her?" mom asked.

"She and Charlie were walking to the grocery store. They waited at the light for it to turn green for them when a car driving out of

245

control swerved and hit them. Charlie, was not hurt but Cindy got the full impact of the car. She has a brain concussion, a punctured lung and a contused heart, a ruptured spleen and liver. Her kidneys are going into renal failure and her heart and blood pressure are being regulated by drugs. "

"Is she conscious?"

"No. We are keeping her in a chemical coma with drugs to keep her cranial pressure down. You can talk to her, but we don't know if she will hear you. I will leave you both alone with Cindy for a little while."

Mom and I were on either side of the bed holding Cindy's hands when Stephanie, Cindy's boss, came in. Within seconds all three of us were crying and hugging each other. The nurse came in and told us Cindy's doctor was making rounds and did we want to talk with him.

"Of course," mom talked for all of us.

"Please follow me to the conference room where you'll have some privacy." We followed the nurse and sat down at the conference table. During the five minutes we waited for the doctor we didn't say a word.

We looked up when a young doctor in scrubs came in. "I am Dr. Harris, the hospitalist doctor assigned to Cindy. I understand that you are her only relatives."

"Dr. Harris, Cindy is my father's caregiver and this is his granddaughter. Stephanie is her boss. Other than that, she doesn't have any family."

"Then let me tell you where we are with Cindy. She is in a coma induced by drugs to keep the pressure in her brain down. She was hit full on by the car and her heart is severely bruised and she has a hole in one lung. We took out her spleen, but we can't take out her liver and she is still bleeding internally. The internal bleeding is causing her kidney failure."

"What are her chances of surviving?" I asked.

"Honestly, they are very low. It hasn't been twenty-four hours since the accident. We will know more in the next forty-eight hours. I am here at the hospital all day and if you wish to talk to me, please have the nurses page me."

"Thank you doctor," we said in unison.

"Oh, Dr. Harris," can my dad, Charlie, come to see her?"

"It is okay with me but you had better check with his caregiver's agency. It may be too traumatic for him." And Dr. Harris went back to his patients.

"What do you think, Stephanie?"

"It's a tough call. Charlie was with Cindy when the accident happened and he no doubt is wondering what happened to her."

"Mom, let's let Charlie decide if he wants to see Cindy in the hospital."

"Darling, that is a wonderful idea. Stephanie, would you like to come home with us? We could use the moral support."

"Of course. I would like to say goodbye to Cindy first."

When we arrived home, Sunny was waiting for us. "Charlie is asleep. How is Cindy?"

We gave Sunny a brief summary of Cindy's condition. "What do you think of Charlie going to the hospital to see Cindy?"

"Well, he was with her when it happened and he is asking how she is."

"Okay, let's ask Charlie when he wakes up," mom took control of what to do.

Grandpa came out of the bedroom just then. "Where's Cindy?"

"Dad, you know that Cindy was hit by a car. We thought it would be a good idea to go see her. What do you think?"

"That's a great idea. Can I bring Dooley along?

We arrived at the hospital thirty minutes later and took the long elevator ride to the Surgical Critical Care Unit. There we identified ourselves through the wall radio to the nurses' station. When grandpa saw Cindy, he broke down in tears. We let him cry for a few minutes and then thought it best if he was taken to the waiting room.

"Dooley wants to stay with Cindy," grandpa said through his tears. Dooley was placed on Cindy's bed and we all left. It was the last time we saw Cindy alive.

Three hours after we got home, mom's cell phone rang. It was the hospital. Cindy had gone into cardiac arrest and with the extensive damage to her heart, she could not be resuscitated. Grandpa was in bed and we decided to wait until morning to tell him.

# Chapter Twelve

Mom and I had some serious decisions to make. "Sally, I just can't leave dad with another new caregiver. He needs time to grieve Cindy before we find someone else."

"I know mom. I've been thinking. See what you think of this plan. We were going to move to Miami, anyway. Can you stay here with grandpa and work on your projects from Miami. I can call the high school principal and let him know our situation. Perhaps I can take my mid-terms on-line. That way we can both be here with grandpa."

"Sally, that is brilliant. Let's make those phone calls tomorrow. I will also call Lorraine, the realtor, and get her to show our place. We don't have many clothes, but we can always take dad on a shopping spree with us."

"Now, that's a brilliant idea," and we both laughed.

Once we got our plan rolling, things fell into place. Mom was working from home and I was doing my school work on-line. Grandpa talked about Cindy every day and on the fifth day, mom and I told him that Cindy had gone with the angels to heaven. He became withdrawn and wouldn't talk. Mom and I had gone back to the hospital to talk with Dr. Harris and the nurses gave us back Dooley.

"Let's give him Dooley and see what happens," mom said. It turns out that this was an excellent idea because Charlie seemed to find a connection with Dooley.

Dr. Harris called us when the autopsy report was back on Cindy.

"I thought you might want to know that Cindy's brain was showing signs of Alzheimer's. If you didn't notice any symptoms of forgetfulness, it was probably because she was a master in covering it up. In a couple more years, she would have been in a memory home."

Mom and I thought the same thing although we didn't talk about it. Was Cindy better off where she is now, or to have lived for who knows how many years in a memory home with no memories of the past.

# Chapter Thirteen

"Darn, these buttons." Charlie muttered to no one in particular. It was just last week that he was the star of the family get together. Now he was a forgetful old man trying to get his shirt buttoned.

Just then, Reggie walked in the room. "Dad what are you muttering about?"

"These gall durn buttons don't go through the hole. Must'a shrunk in the dryer. Mother always said that the sun is the best way to dry clothes."

"Here Dad. Let me help you." Reggie unbuttoned the buttons that were in unfamiliar button holes, straightened up his shirt and then systematically lined up the buttons and inserted them into the correct button holes one by one. "I have an idea. When we come back from your doctor's appointment, we'll stop and get you some pull over shirts. You know we never got them the last time we talked. Then you won't need to worry about buttons.

"I have worn a buttoned shirt for the past sixty years. Why when I was working at the factory on airplanes, I worn a clean, white shirt and tie go to work. These young kids today don't know a thing about lookin' nice. Here, why am I dressed in my good shirt?

"Dad, you have a doctor's appointment. Remember we go to see Dr. George every month."

"Now why in tarnation do I need to see a doctor?"

Reggie knew it would do no good to explain to her dad about

251

his progressing Alzheimer disease. "Come on dad, or we'll be late."

Charlie dutifully followed his daughter from the bedroom into the kitchen. "Where is the coffee?" Charlie asked. "Dad, we don't have time for coffee.

"I'll get you a cup when we get to the clinic."

"Why are we going to the clinic? I'm not sick."

"Let's go, dad."

Grandpa stood in the middle of the kitchen. "Reggie, I saw Cindy last night."

Mom and I turned to look at him. "What do you mean, Dad?"

"I saw Cindy. She looked like an angel and she kept motioning for me to follow her. It was so peaceful and Cindy was so beautiful."

Mom and I didn't know what to say and told grandpa that we needed to get going.

The next morning, grandpa didn't come out of his bedroom when we usually expected him. When I went in to check on him, he was lying in bed fully clothed and Dooley was in his arms. Next to the bed on the nightstand was a short note written in Charlie's handwriting

*'I've gone with Cindy where there is no forgetfulness or fear.'*

"Mom, do you think Cindy was real, or was she was an angel sent to take Charlie to the next world."

"Who knows, sweetheart. There is only one person who can tell us."

"Who is that?"

"Just Charlie."

# Epilogue

"Cindy is that you?" Charlie asked when he saw his angel.

"Yes, Charlie, it's me and I'm glad that you have come to the other side to join me."

"I remember that we were hit by a car and you died. Did you have much pain?"

"No Charlie, I had my share of pain when I was a human on earth the first time."

"I don't want to forget and be afraid. Will that happen to me here?"

"No, Charlie. You will never again forget or be afraid. You will only know the kindness and love of all eternity. Soon Reggie and Sally will join you. But for now, let's join those who have passed to the other side ahead of you.

Cindy took Charlie's hand, and they began their journey on the other side.

Did this really happen?

Just Charlie knows.

# Moonbeams and Fireflies

A Small Compilation of Love Poems

# Our Love

We met and fell in love,
Each day shines like the stars above.
A purpose to life we have rendered,
Togetherness is ours to surrender.

Lovers and best friends we are,
Nights and love came from afar.
We share a special tenderness,
To be together is measureless.

Love tonight is ours,
Our love reaches to the stars.
All too soon you were taken from me,
And I was left alone and adrift on the sea.

# Some Say

Love doesn't come along every day,
It's why it's so special some say.
Love has a silent kindred heart,
A love some say that cannot part.

Love shares untold desires,
Words some say are not required.
Love knows no restraints or borders,
It's why some say there is no disorder.

Love is silent and there for the other,
Knowing when to talk some say and when not to bother.
My love came into my life today,
A special place he holds in my heart I would say.

# First Anniversarry

We met a year ago and fell in love,
Each star shines brightly from above.
A purpose to life you have given me,
For together we were meant to be.

We are best friends and lovers,
What a wonderful life discovered.
Our love was easy to declare,
Ours was an enviable love affair.

We married on the deck of a yacht,
With nary a person as mascot.
Today on our first anniversary,
I vow to love you into eternity

Sandra Bobbitt

# Broken Heart

Your heart was broken,
Doctors left words unspoken.
Surgery did not fix your heart,
You began dying from the start

Words we did not speak,
Your body too weak.
For days you lay in the hospital,
Recovery information too little.

I sat by your side in silence,
Waiting for someone with guidance.
How many tests could you endure?
What would bring a cure?

Your body was tired and worn,
Your will to live torn.
It was time for you to leave,
It was time for me to grieve.

# Angels Came For You

It is dark outside and I yearn for night,
Nighttime brings me solitude.
At night your pains reach out to me,
My soul aches with my love for you.

My love for you is endless,
Yet we are not together.
The angels came to take you,
And left me alone and crying.

# I Am Lonesome

I am lonesome,
You have gone from my heart.
You didn't say goodbye,
My tears won't let you go.

You were my love, my best friend,
Our love we shared together.
Now you are gone,
And my heart is broken.

# Calls of the Earth

Phantoms of the night call upon me,
Winds of the sky murmur to me.
Fires of the earth send fury to me,
Solitudes of being overcome me.

Their longings shout to me,
Their songs call to me.
Their biddings whimper to me,
Their calls of death overcome me.

The yearnings of the earth beckon to me,
Longings and cries frighten me.
Their power is daunting to me,
When will they leave me?

# Moonbeams and Fireflies

There are no words to help with sorrow,
Days are filled with sadness today and tomorrow.
A special gift to have loved one so dear,
That love is captured with each shed tear.

Know that you will always be in my heart,
For by knowing we will never be apart.
I only need to think of your presence,
To know you are with me is the essence.

I mourn your death as a seagull traverses the sea,
You gave me moonbeams and fireflies to guide me.
In life you gave me your love and compassion,
In death I give you tears, memories and passion.

# The Search for Love

Night is followed by dawn's light,
Dreams bring hope of love in sight.
Why does one live and another die?
These are questions of why.

Why did my beloved go away?
Why do I find emptiness each day?
Why does nighttime bring solitude?
Why do I long for love renewed?

The loss of love is followed by hope.
Days are filled with the struggle to cope.
Yearning another love will come my way,
Looking for love is a search each day.

# The Eagle Soars

I pause to hear your piercing cry,
High on massive wings you fly.
Temptation lures below the sky,
You seek what yonder lies.

You are a Messenger of flight,
Master of days and night.
Voyager of all that is right,
Minstrel of adventure and light.

I am a traveler of the earth,
Seeking mysteries of birth.
Whodunit clues have mystery and worth,
Tales of adventure and mirth.

Your shadows call upon me.
Your winds whisper to me,
I love to hear your piercing cry,
Adventures in the sky.

# Nature's Songs

The wind blows over the plains,
Water falls from the sky with rain.
Fires burn in a heated dance,
These sounds remind me of our romance.

I long for the wind in my hair,
To walk on the beach without care.
To watch a fire with fascination,
To fly into the sunset with reincarnation

# My Special Stars

There are stars to take us up in the sky,
Adventures are ours to have flying high.
I've searched for my special star,
The star that took my love so far.

Will I ever find that star again?
Will I ever love again?
I wait and watch the star-studded sky,
Waiting for that special star to fly by.

# Alone at Christmas

It is time for the holidays and cheer,
People meet with those who are dear.
Carols are sung and children play,
For me it is just another day.

Snow is falling and children sing,
What wonders the season brings.
Church bells ring in the night,
Christmas is coming tonight.

I put up a tree adorned with lights,
Mistletoe is not there at night.
There are no presents under the tree,
All I want is company.

I watch from my window with envy,
I want to be in a crowd of frenzy.
Slowly I close the curtains and sigh,
Another Christmas alone am I.

# The World Was Mine to Have

The world was mine to have,
didn't know where I'd been.
I searched the world for love,
My heart and dreams are empty.

I searched the world for you,
And one day you appeared.
We fell in love completely,
And my heart and dreams are smiling.

# A Life Once Shared

A sunset, a sunrise,
An ocean breeze,
A mountain top,
Or a desert scene.

Experiencing life,
Only becomes true,
When sharing with one,
Was all I knew.

Standing on a porch,
Driving down a road,
Viewing from a cliff,
What are we bestowed?

Sharing makes us one,
No words need spoken,
Thoughts are shared,
Minds are cherished tokens.

Days and nights are lost,
There is no one for sharing.
This leaves me empty,

Sandra Bobbitt

I so wish for caring.

I once had fulfillment,
A mate that was there.
Sunrises and sunsets,
Filled with love and care.

My beloved husband died,
I am left with a broken heart.
I've no one to share my life,
I'm broken into shattered parts.

# Widowhood

Widowhood is unexpected.
It's a time of loneliness.
It's a time of grieving
It's a time for reflection.
It's a renewal of who we are.

We wonder how to be single again.
How to find new friends.
How to learn to let go.
How to love again.
How to go on living.

# You Are Here

You are here I know,
Be the softness of fallen snow.
Like angel wings upon the wind,
My fairy tale story has no end.

I feel you with me in the night,
When loneliness waits for light.
Your shadows are wisps of cotton,
Your whispers are unforgotten.

Your smile is forever with me,
Your love has set me free.
You are here I know,
Waiting for my time to go.

# The Final Love Story

This is the story of two people so in
love they could not be apart.

"Who are you?" he asked. "And where am I?"
She took his withered hand and smiled at his kind face.
"I am your wife, and you are home,"
Where you have always been.
I remember now, he said.

He lay his head back in her lap.
Soon he looked at her and asked, "What is your name?"
He fell asleep in the comfort of her touch,
She remembered when they were young.
They were so in love and never separated.

Suddenly she knew something was wrong.
He became still and his breathing had stopped,
with tears running down her face she cradled his head,
"You can't leave me now; I need you by my side.
" But he would never awaken again.

She dried her eyes and knew she would soon join him.
Laying down beside him she nestled him in her arms.

Sandra Bobbitt

When they met on the other side,
He looked at her with all the love in his heart.
"I remember you, you are my wife and I love you."

# Epilogue

I am an ordinary woman who has had an incredible life. It has not been without love, loss, trauma, tears, sorrow, laughter, or incident. I was married for twenty-five wonderful years that ended all too soon when my late husband became ill with a terminal illness. I have learned how to be single again in my retirement years; not always an easy task. However, as I grow older, life has taken on a new meaning as I embrace who I am and what I have to offer to the world.

I thank all of the people that have come and gone in my life giving me love, support and meaning to each day.

CPSIA information can be obtained
at www.ICGtesting.com
Printed in the USA
LVHW100407171122
733336LV00029B/736

9 781998 784622